FOUL DEEDS & SUSPICIOUS DEATHS AROUND HUDDERSFIELD

FOUL DEEDS AND SUSPICIOUS DEATHS Series

Wharncliffe's *Foul Deeds and Suspicious Deaths* series explores, in detail, crimes of passion, brutal murders and foul misdemeanours from early modern times to the present day. Victorian street crime, mysterious deaths and modern murders tell tales where passion, jealousy and social deprivation brought unexpected violence to those involved. From unexplained death and suicide to murder and manslaughter, the books provide a fascinating insight into the lives of both victims and perpetrators as well as society as a whole.

Other titles in the series include:

Foul Deeds and Suspicious Deaths in Bolton, Glynis Cooper
ISBN: 1-903425-63-8. £9.99

Foul Deeds and Suspicious Deaths in London's East End, Geoffrey Howse
ISBN: 1-903425-71-9. £10.99

Foul Deeds and Suspicious Deaths in & around Durham, Maureen Anderson
ISBN: 1-903425-46-8. £9.99

Foul Deeds and Suspicious Deaths in Hampstead, Holburn & St Pancras, Mark Aston
ISBN: 1-903425-94-8. £10.99

Foul Deeds and Suspicious Deaths in Colchester, Patrick Denney
ISBN: 1-903425-80-8. £10.99

Foul Deeds and Suspicious Deaths in Newport, Terry Underwood
ISBN: 1-903425-59-X. £9.99

Foul Deeds and Suspicious Deaths Around Derby, Kevin Turton
ISBN: 1-903425-76-X. £9.99

Foul Deeds and Suspicious Deaths in and Around Scunthorpe, Stephen Wade
ISBN: 1-903425-88-3. £9.99

More Foul Deeds and Suspicious Deaths in Wakefield, Kate Taylor
ISBN: 1-903425-48-4. £9.99

Foul Deeds and Suspicious Deaths in York, Keith Henson
ISBN: 1-903425-33-6. £9.99

Foul Deeds and Suspicious Deaths on the Yorkshire Coast, Alan Whitworth
ISBN: 1-903425-01-8. £9.99

Foul Deeds and Suspicious Deaths in Coventry, David McGrory
ISBN: 1-903425-57-3. £9.99

Foul Deeds and Suspicious Deaths in Manchester, Martin Baggoley
ISBN: 1-903425-65-4. £9.99

Foul Deeds and Suspicious Deaths in Newcastle, Maureen Anderson
ISBN: 1-903425-34-4. £9.99

Foul Deeds and Suspicious Deaths in Hull, David Goodman
ISBN: 1-903425-43-3. £9.99

Foul Deeds and Suspicious Deaths Around Newport, Terry Underwood
ISBN: 1-903425-59-X. £9.99

Please contact us via any of the methods below for more information or a catalogue.
WHARNCLIFFE BOOKS
47 Church Street – Barnsley – South Yorkshire S70 2AS
Tel: 01226 734555 – 734222; Fax: 01226 724438
E-mail: enquiries@pen-and-sword.co.uk
Website: www.wharncliffebooks.co.uk

Foul Deeds & Suspicious Deaths Around

HUDDERSFIELD

VIVIEN TEASDALE

Series Editor
Brian Elliott

Wharncliffe Books

First Published in Great Britain in 2007 by
Wharncliffe Books
an imprint of
Pen and Sword Books Ltd
47 Church Street
Barnsley
South Yorkshire
S70 2AS

Copyright © Vivien Teasdale 2007

ISBN: 978-184563-039-4

Typeset in 10/12pt Plantin by Concept, Huddersfield.

Printed and bound in England by Biddles.

Pen and Sword Books Ltd incorporates the Imprints of
Pen & Sword Aviation, Pen & Sword Maritime,
Pen & Sword Military, Wharncliffe Books,
Pen & Sword Select, Pen and Sword Military Classics
and Leo Cooper.

For a complete list of Pen & Sword titles please contact
PEN & SWORD BOOKS LIMITED
47 Church Street
Barnsley
South Yorkshire
S70 2BR
England
E-mail: enquiries@pen-and-sword.co.uk
Website: www.pen-and-sword.co.uk

Contents

Introduction and Acknowledgements

In 1801 the population of Huddersfield was around 7,000. Twenty years later this had almost doubled and continued to grow throughout the nineteenth century. Not surprisingly this rapid increase in population brought with it an equally rapid increase in crime. Poor working conditions, poor living conditions and relatively easily available alcohol exacerbated the situation. Yet if we read current papers, the stories are not so different. Perhaps that is what makes crime stories so fascinating – the dark side of human life always seems to be with us.

All crimes are heard first of all in the magistrates' court. They may then be dealt with if they fall within the jurisdiction of that court, or be passed on to the Crown Court if they are more serious crimes. Many Huddersfield criminals found themselves being sent to York gaol – and ultimately hanged there too. Later, Armley gaol in Leeds and eventually Wakefield gaol became the principal recipient of the worst offenders, where many were hanged. Some were kept in the prisons awaiting transportation, initially to the hulks – ships moored offshore where prisoners could be kept before being sent off to distant parts of the empire. Those who were declared insane were supposed to be moved to 'lunatic asylums' but often remained in prison for long periods or even for life. Although the asylums improved over the years, conditions were in many cases quite barbaric by our standards.

In researching the stories told here, my biggest problem was deciding what to leave out. I have included some well known cases, such as the killing of William Horsfall, some which caused a sensation but have since been almost forgotten and others which merely warranted a short paragraph at the time but which seemed particularly poignant to me, such as the death of John Herbert Cooke. All the cases I read, both those printed here and those omitted, proved a fascinating insight into the changing attitudes of society towards young offenders, women – particularly those who had recently given birth and subsequently disposed of their children – and violence generally, and particularly when accompanied by drink. Habitual offenders received no sympathy whatsoever and if you were wrongly accused, well, having your name cleared was sufficient, there was no 'compensation culture' then.

Magistrates' Court, Huddersfield, 2006. The Author

In producing this book, I have to thank the staff at both Kirklees Library and Archives Services and Wakefield Library and Archives Services for their unfailing willingness to help and offer advice on sources available. Thanks also to Brian Elliott at Pen & Sword Books Ltd for his continued assistance and help in getting the details from note form to publishable copy and, as always, to my family and friends for their generous encouragement and support.

CHAPTER 1

Without Due Care
1811

... to judge whether the accident arose from the carelessness of the driver or the indiscretion of the deceased.

Accidents do happen. There have often been cases of drivers forgetting the handbrake, and then seeing their car roll away down the road, causing havoc en route. But at least the car doesn't have a mind of its own. A horse is a different matter.

On Thursday 10 January 1811, John Garside (or Gartside), the post boy from the Rose and Crown Inn, set his passengers down at the inn and decided he would go for some refreshment himself. Unfortunately, there was no one around to look after the chaise and horses, but they seemed quiet enough and he did not intend to be long. He left the carriage at the door and went inside.

But something spooked the horses and they 'set off at full speed down King Street'. At the same time, Hannah Mellor had set off to cross the road. The carriage hit the girl, who was only fifteen, knocking her down onto the cobbled road and killed her.

The horses 'pursuing their unrestrained course' were finally captured and taken back to the Rose and Crown.

The next day an inquest returned a verdict of manslaughter against John Garside who was taken to York Castle to await trial at the Lent Assizes.

Mr Barrow prosecuted, accusing Garside of carelessness in leaving 'his chaise without a person to take care of the horses'. However, other witnesses, whilst agreeing that Garside had left his horses, stated that 'instantly an alarm being given, the prisoner followed them and brought them back again'.

Ann Allison agreed, saying that 'when the prisoner had brought back the chaise he turned the heads of the horses down the street. The prisoner again left the horses and was going towards the house, when

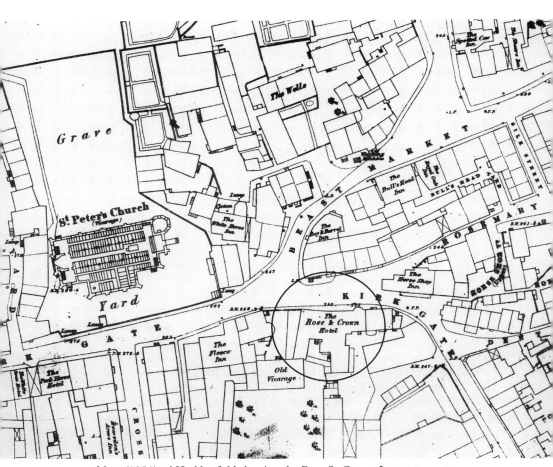

Map (1851) of Huddersfield showing the Rose & Crown Inn. Ordnance Survey

the horses set off at a great rate down the street.' Allison went on to say that there had been a number of girls nearby and Garside had 'told the girls that were standing there that if they would wait until he came out of the house he would treat them to a ride'.

William Charters also saw the horses going down the street but then lost sight of the chaise for a short time; when he saw it again the wheel of the chaise had just passed over the deceased 'who immediately stretched herself out and never seemed to move afterwards'.

Mr Rowland Hough, surgeon, went on to describe the nature of the injury done to the deceased which caused her immediate death. However, the judge commented that 'it would have been more satisfactory if the precise manner in which the chaise came into contact with the deceased had been described as the jury would then have been better able to judge whether the accident arose from the carelessness of the driver or the indiscretion of the deceased. They would however take into consideration all the circumstances that had been given in evidence and if they were convinced that the deceased came by her death through the want of proper care in the prisoner they would find him guilty but if they had any reasonable doubts on the subject they would in that case acquit him.'

The jury retired, eventually agreeing on a verdict of 'not guilty'.

Hannah, the daughter of George Mellor, was buried in the Huddersfield St Peter's churchyard.

CHAPTER 2

Death and Disturbances 1812

The local magistrates and mill owners were determined to stamp out any possibility of revolution.

This must be one of the most famous murder cases in Huddersfield's history. It marked a turning point in the attitude of both the authorities and of the workers.

At the beginning of the nineteenth century croppers were skilled, highly paid workmen. By the end of the same century, their job was non-existent – it had been taken over by machinery. In the intervening years, there had been much suffering, much painful adjustment and many bloody incidents.

The French Revolution in 1789 horrified many of the ruling classes in Britain. They were terrified that a similar event could happen here, and any suggestion of political ideas amongst the population at large caused panic. War between Britain and France made matters even worse. Napoleon's Continental System, aimed at blockading Britain's ports and preventing trade, caused many prices to rise, hitting the working classes hardest. Combined with a series of poor harvests, thousands were starving and discontent – a situation ripe for revolution.

At the same time, mechanisation in the textile industry had begun, with spinning machines, power-looms and knitting-frames becoming widespread, a process that began to put men out of work. Riots began in the Midlands where knitting-frames were smashed. A joking reference to their leader, a Ned Ludd (who was in fact a young lad of limited intelligence) stuck and the rioters became known as Luddites. By 1812 the disturbances had spread to the North.

Mills and workshops were attacked; homes were raided for arms and 'contributions' from the terrified families. The men appeared to be fairly well organised and many were sworn or 'twisted' in to secrecy. The local magistrates and mill owners were determined to stamp out any possibility of revolution. The local militia were called

The Dumb Steeple where the Luddites rallied before their attack on Rawfolds Mill.
The Author

out and troops were sent from other parts of the country. There was a state of siege in the area.

On 11 April 1812 Rawfolds Mill not far from Dewsbury was attacked by a large gang of men. Its owner, William Cartwright, was ready for the attack, guarding the mill with armed men and soldiers. An alarm bell on the roof alerted yet more soldiers stationed nearby and Cartwright had placed spiked rollers on the stairs, which could be

Bank Bottom Mills covering some of the site of Ottiwells Mill. The Author

released onto the men below. A large tub of acid was kept ready too in case the men succeeded in breaking into the mill.

The Luddites assembled by a stone obelisk known locally as the Dumb Steeple then set off in formation for the mill. The attack lasted only twenty minutes, at the end of which two Luddites were mortally injured and many badly wounded. The inquest decided this was 'justifiable homicide'. When it was known what had awaited them, had they succeeded in getting into the mill, the anger of the workmen boiled over. Up to that point they had avoided bloodshed, yet now two of their friends were dead. They vowed to have revenge.

Seven days later there was an attempted assassination of William Cartwright but the shots missed.

But there was another target. William Horsfall owned Ottiwells Mill in Marsden – later to be demolished – and Bank Bottom Mills built on the same site – and was known to be an implacable enemy of the Luddites. On Tuesday 28 April, he went, as was his custom, to the weekly market in Huddersfield. He set off around 5 pm, stopping at the Warren House Inn in Crosland Moor for refreshment. Setting off once more for home, he had barely gone 300 yards, when shots rang out and he fell forward onto his horse's neck. Others rushed to his aid, and he was taken back to the inn. A surgeon attended but the shots

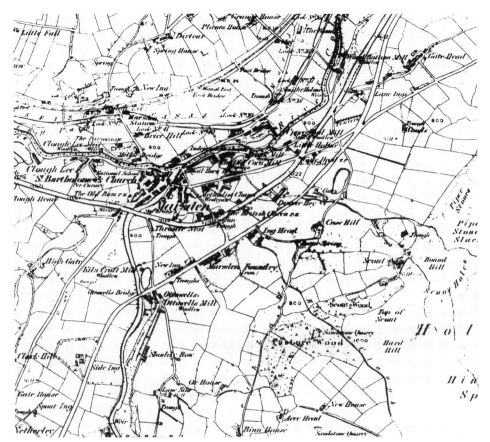

Map (1854) of Marsden showing site of Ottiwells Mill owned by Horsfall. Ordnance Survey

had severed the femoral artery in his right thigh and though he lingered until Thursday morning, it was obvious nothing could be done. He was buried four days later on 4 May at the parish church, Huddersfield. A witness, and Horsfall himself, said they had seen four men running from the scene. Troops from the Queen's Bays were soon on the scene and searching the area, but could find no trace of the men. A reward of £2,000 was offered for information.

Initially suspicion fell on Samuel Haigh of Totties, but the evidence against him proved spurious. For months the authorities were unable to break through the wall of secrecy in the area, until a cloth-dresser called Benjamin Walker, unable to read but eventually hearing of the £2,000 reward, sent his mother to the magistrate, Joseph Radcliffe, with information. Walker turned King's Evidence but even he was probably not expecting to be quickly removed to Chester Castle, where he was held for ten weeks before finally appearing at the trial. He had been held and interrogated for four days prior to removal, by John Lloyd, a solicitor and clerk to one of the Stockport magistrates. Lloyd was rumoured to use torture to extract the information he wanted, so it is not surprising that Walker named names. He confessed that he was one of the four men, the other three being George Mellor, William Thorpe and Thomas Smith.

The trial took place in York, presided over by Sir Alexander Thompson and Sir Simon Le Blanc. The three prisoners all pleaded 'not guilty' and were defended by Henry Brougham, later Chancellor of England.

According to the prosecution, both Horsfall and a witness, Henry Parr, saw four men together in the plantation near the Warren House inn. However, Henry Parr began his statement by saying that he was returning home from Huddersfield 'when he came near the Warrener House, I heard the report of fire arms; I saw the smoke and I saw four persons in the plantation from which I was about 150 yards.' On cross-examination he stated that 'his attention was drawn to the place where he heard the report; he saw four men together at the corner of the plantation nearest to Huddersfield; the plantation is only about thirty yards over.'

Yet on re-examination by the prosecution, he stated that he saw the four walking about in the plantation, and that he saw them before he 'heard the crack'. When he got up to the plantation, one of them stooped under a bough and fired a piece (a gun), the other three standing behind him. His evidence had changed considerably in this time.

Rowland Houghton, the surgeon who had treated Horsfall, said that there were 'Two wounds in the upper part of the left thigh about three inches asunder, another in the lower part of the belly on the left side, another on the lower part of the scrotum and two more on the right thigh and a slight bruise, not a wound on the lower part of the belly.' He continued: 'I extracted one large musket ball from the outside of the right thigh, near the hip joint. Gave the ball to Mr Horsfall's brother, the Reverend Abraham Horsfall.'

This suggests that Horsfall was hit by a number of bullets. There appear to have been at least four hits on the left, and possibly two on the right. The wounds on the right may have been exit wounds but if not it suggests that more people were involved and firing from different positions.

Next came the damning evidence of Benjamin Walker. Walker, Mellor and Smith all worked at John Wood's cropping shop in Longroyd Bridge, whilst Thorpe worked for Mr Fisher, nearby. Walker said that the men had discussed the attack on Cartwright's mill and Mellor had said, 'The method of breaking shears must be given up and instead of it, the masters must be shot.' Sometime between 4 and 5 pm on the day Horsfall was shot, Mellor, Smith, Thorpe, William Hall, Ben Walker's father and brother, William, as well as Ben himself, met together. Mellor asked Ben if he would go with him to shoot Horsfall, and then Ben went drinking, returning half an hour later. Mellor was still there, with James Varley and Hall. Mellor gave Ben Walker a loaded pistol, saying he must go with him and shoot Horsfall. Smith and Walker went off together, both having a loaded pistol. At that time he admitted Mellor was 'dressed in a drab coloured jacket' but when he got to the plantation he was wearing a 'bottle green top coat'. Thorpe was wearing 'a dark top coat', whilst Smith and Walker wore 'close-bodied bottle green coats'. They arrived at the plantation ten minutes before the other two and, according to Walker, began to have doubts, both wanting to back out. Smith went up to Mellor and Thorpe when they arrived, but soon returned, telling Walker that if they attempted to leave, they would be shot. Mellor's pistol, which he had brought back from Russia, was described as having a 'barrel of . . . nearly half a yard long'. Once in the wood, Walker and Smith were told to stand about twenty yards away from Mellor and Thorpe, who were at the corner of the plantation nearest the Warren House. They were to fire if the first two missed. Walker said he could not see the other two so could not confirm what they did. They heard the pistol go off and fled further into the wood, soon joined by Mellor and Thorpe who were angry that neither of their conspirators had fired. Thorpe thrust his pistol at Walker, saying he wouldn't carry it any further and it was then that Walker noticed that the barrel was warm and the cock of the gun was down.

The men ran off into Dungeon Wood, Walker throwing down Thorpe's gun, which Mellor picked up. Smith and Walker hid their guns in the wood, before setting off for Honley. Mellor had instructed them to go there, giving Walker two shillings (10p) for drinks. The two men then went off to Honley, and were still there drinking when a man came in and mentioned Horsfall being shot. The landlady, Mary Robinson, remembered them, saying that they arrived between 7 and 8 pm. Walker left around 9 pm, arriving home an hour later. The following day, Mellor sent his friend Joseph Sowden to fetch Walker to the shop in Longroyd Bridge where all were sworn to secrecy. Mellor had an injured finger, which he said was from firing the gun –

Beaumont Park, Huddersfield which incorporates part of Dungeon Wood. The Author

he had loaded it with double shot; Thorpe's face was cut and bloody where he had run through the wood.

On cross-examination, Walker pointed out that, although people could see Mellor and Thorpe in the plantation, no one could see himself and Smith since they were further into the wood. There was also a high wall around the plantation and the two men lay down behind it. This contradicts Parr's statement of seeing four men in the wood – unless there were many others involved. Walker specifically states that they were 'never all four together in the nook [corner] of the plantation'.

William Hall was next called to confirm that he had lent Mellor the pistol. Hall had bought it from 'a man' at Mirfield Moor, but it was the same gun that Mellor had brought from Russia and sold on to a Richard Hartley, who must then have also sold the gun elsewhere. It had an iron end, screws at the side and a barrel about a foot long. Hall saw Mellor load the gun – 'he put nearly two pipe-heads full of fine powder into it, and then a ball and some slugs which he beat out with a hammer from balls, and put two or three in and then put a ball in the top and rammed them all down'. Hall also saw Thorpe with a pistol and heard Walker agreeing to go to shoot Horsfall. He too was sworn to secrecy the day after the shooting. The gun was finally returned to him three weeks later by James Varley, but then Mellor had asked him to send it to some men in Leeds and he had agreed. Mellor had also asked Hall to take Thorpe's coat and go with him before Mr Radcliffe the magistrate and pretend to have been with Mellor to his cousins', saying he had been looking for work, but Hall, whilst agreeing at first, thought better of this in case he was mistaken for the murderer. On being cross-examined, Hall did not 'recollect meeting either James Harper or Joseph Rushworth and saying to them he had cleared Walker by showing that he was not at the place when the murder happened'. Neither of these men were mentioned again – who were they? Could they have cleared Mellor and Thorpe?

Joseph Sowden, cloth-dresser, confirmed that he saw the meeting at 4 or 5 pm in John Wood's shop. Ben Walker, John Walker, his son William, William Hall and Varley were all there. He heard Mellor order Ben Walker to go home and fetch top coats and a pistol. Sowden, after being threatened, was sworn to secrecy next morning.

Abraham Willie, a workman of Mr Radcliffe, said he was in a building working with horses when he saw four men running from the plantation towards Dungeon Wood. He was within fifty yards of them and they were all in dark clothing.

Edward Hartley, who was coming from Crosland to Lockwood that evening, also saw four men running out of Mr Radcliffe's field jump over the wall and run towards Dungeon Wood: 'They were all dressed in dark clothes; he saw the brass end of a pistol from under the coat of one of them; witness made an observation about seeing the pistol to a person who was with him which he supposes must have been heard as the man who held it immediately covered it with his top coat.' The 'person' was not called as a witness to corroborate this.

Map (1854) showing Dungeon Wood. Ordnance Survey

Then Martha Mellor, wife of Joseph Mellor and cousin of George, who lived in Dungeon Bottom, near Dungeon Wood, was questioned. They had one child, four apprentice boys and a servant girl, though Joseph Holdham, one of the apprentices, had suddenly left employment for misbehaviour one week after Mellor had been committed to York. Martha's statement was reported as:

> *I saw Mellor in the afternoon of the day of the murder, about 6.15 pm. There was a gentleman with him then, whom I have not seen since. They came from the workshop into the house. George asked if my husband was in. I told him he was at market. He then asked me if we wanted a man to work. I told him we had no occasion. He asked me to lend him a handkerchief and I lent him a black silk one. He asked me if I would allow the gentleman to wash himself. He had light coloured stockings, light coloured waistcoat, and light coloured breeches and he had not then a great coat on, he had put it off. The other person had a great coat. George asked to borrow a coat and I told him my master's coat was in the shop. They stopped about a quarter of an hour.*

Martha said that she had worked out the time because her husband had returned about 7 pm. This contrasts with the statement by the apprentice, Thomas Durrance, aged seventeen, who said that his master had returned home about an hour and a half after the two men had left. If his master had indeed returned around 7 pm, then the visitors must have been there at about 5.30 pm not 6.15 pm. If Durrance was correct, Mellor could not have been in the plantation shooting at Horsfall. Yet according to Durrance, Mellor had hidden pistols in the flocks in the workhouse, which later Durrance and his master took and hid in the barn. Martha Mellor's description of the 'gentleman' with Mellor does not fit with the 'men in black' seen in the plantation. A top coat would not cover all the light coloured clothes underneath, especially not when jumping over a four feet high wall. Who was this man with Mellor? He does not appear to have been anyone Martha knew or recognised in court, yet apparently he did not appear as defence witness. Why not?

Durrance was later given five shillings (25p) by Mellor to share with John Kinder and told not to say anything about the pistols.

John Kinder, aged eighteen, did not know Mellor, but agreed that he saw the pistols in the flock room. They might have been empty but he wasn't sure. He confirmed receiving half a crown from Durrance.

Joseph Mellor, George Mellor's cousin, said he left Huddersfield at 6 pm and got home about 7 pm. Durrance showed him the two pistols that they then hid under some straw for fear the pistols would be found on the premises. One of them had a larger bore than the other. On returning home, he found a dark top coat, with two balls in the pocket and next morning he found a dark green top coat, neither of which belonged to him. His coat was a light drab coat, which was missing.

This closed the case for the prosecution, and allowed the defence to produce their alibis.

First, William Hanson stated that he saw Mellor near Huddersfield going to Longroyd Bridge at 6.45 pm. Next, John Womersley, a clock and watchmaker, saw Mellor at 6.15 pm in Huddersfield at the corner of Cloth Hall Street. Since Mellor owed him seven shillings (35p) for some work Womersley had done for him, they went to Mr Taverner's White Hart (now known as the Hart Inn) and stopped about twenty minutes. Mellor stopped there with William Battersby while Womersley then went on to the Brown Cow and had just arrived there when he heard the news of Horsfall's shooting.

William Battersby agreed he saw Mellor and Womersley at the White Hart, and had two pints of ale with them. Womersley left first, and the others stayed drinking for a further half hour. Battersby parted with Mellor at the door after they had heard of the shooting.

The Hart, Huddersfield which used to be the White Hart Inn. The Author

John Thorpe, who lived in Castle Street in Huddersfield swore he saw Mellor in Huddersfield near the George Inn around 5.50 pm. Thorpe had a watch which he wanted to sell to Mellor. They had both looked at the watch, which Thorpe valued at £3 13s (£3.65) but Mellor refused to buy it.

Jonathan Battersby (the records do not state whether he was any relation to William Battersby) saw Mr Horsfall setting off from Huddersfield. Battersby then went home and got his tea before putting on his coat and walking up the street. This took about twenty minutes. It was at that point he saw Mellor and they chatted for a few minutes before he returned home, where he heard of Horsfall's shooting.

George Armitage, blacksmith, living at Lockwood saw Mellor go past Lockwood Bar towards Huddersfield between 5 and 6 pm. Sometimes the men go 'to their drinking' earlier, but this day they had been detained by work and it was nearer 5.30 pm. Mellor told the blacksmith he had been at Joseph Mellor's with a man wanting work. Joseph Armitage, his brother, confirmed the time.

Charles Ratcliffe, a cloth-dresser from Huddersfield was at Mr Fisher's of Longroyd Bridge in the raising shop at 5.30 pm, seeking work. He did not see Fisher, only Thorpe, whom he knew and 'saw

The original George Hotel, Huddersfield. The Author

him raising a blue coat piece there'. Whilst they were talking, a young woman came in for water out of the raising shop. Ratcliffe arrived in Huddersfield about 6.20 pm by the Cloth Hall clock.

Frances Midwood, of Longroyd Bridge, kept her father's house and, as usual drank tea around 4.30 pm. As the next day was washing day she went to get water from the raising house at about 5 pm. The first time she saw no one, next time she went, about ten minutes later she saw Thorpe and the third time saw some other person was with him. She continued fetching water until she heard of Horsfall's shooting. One time she saw Abraham Pilling, shoemaker, who was bringing her some new shoes and he followed her in to the shop, where he stayed talking to Thorpe. On cross-examination she couldn't remember who had first asked what time she took tea, but thought it had been Mr Blackburn, the prisoner's attorney.

Abraham Pilling, shoemaker, agreed that he took some new shoes for Frances Midwood to her house and followed her to the raising shop where they found Thorpe. Pilling told Frances the price of the shoes and she went and fetched a guinea note belonging to Ingham's bank. It was 5.45 pm when he set off from home and he lived about a

Clock from the Cloth Hall, Huddersfield, now in Ravensknowle Park. The Author

mile from Longroyd Bridge. He remained about half an hour before setting off for Marsh, a mile further on, but as he came out of the raising house, he was told about the shooting.

John Bower, aged seventeen and an apprentice to Mr Wood of Longroyd Bridge told the court that Mellor, who was also John Wood's stepson, supervised their work. Mellor was there in the afternoon, helping with the pressing. Thomas Smith, Ben Walker, James Varley and John Walker were also there and it was near 7 pm. He was quite sure Smith was there too as he was also an apprentice.

William Hall confirmed that Widow Harley brought news of the shooting about 7 pm. It was a particularly busy day and they did not go to their drinking till around 6 pm and it was after that they heard the news.

William Hirst of Longroyd Bridge remembered Ben Walker being there in Wood's shop when news of the shooting came in but the counsel for the Crown objected to his evidence since it consisted of what Ben Walker had said. This objection was sustained and Hirst merely confirmed that he had been there and left around 6.40 pm.

Joseph Rushworth of Cowcliffe, confirmed knowing that Hall had been examined by Mr Ratcliffe.

The summing up reiterated the prosecution evidence, stressing 'the conduct of Mr Horsfall, in manfully opposing the system of depredation and outrage which was so unhappily prevalent in that district'.

The jury withdrew, but took only twenty minutes to consider the 'justice of the case' before bringing in a verdict of guilty against all the prisoners.

When asked if they had anything to say why sentence of death should not be passed on them, Mellor replied, 'I have nothing to say, but that I am not guilty.' Thorpe said, 'I am not guilty, false evidence has been given against me' whilst Smith simply stated, 'Not guilty.'

The judge, before pronouncing sentence, stressed that they had not been convicted on the testimony of Walker but 'by a chain of circumstances which do not depend on his testimony, nor on the testimony of any two or three witnesses and some of the most material circumstances against you are established by witnesses who, if they had not been honest in a certain degree would have given a different testimony. Of your guilt there can be no doubt.'

Yet there can be considerable doubt. Initial accusations were made about a man called Samuel Haigh, who was quickly released. Joshua Haigh, a private in the 51st Regiment of Foot was also arrested and charged 'with being concerned with others, in murdering William Horsfall . . .' but was later released.

When Ben Walker first confessed he said, 'Mr Mellor fired two pistols and Thorpe one, either Smith or himself fired . . .' At no point was it brought out in the trial that Mellor had two pistols and surely Walker should know whether he fired a pistol or not! Later he changed this statement, saying that only Mellor and Thorpe fired. It is also significant that Walker only agreed to testify against the others when he heard about the £2,000 reward.

There are a number of anomalies and contradictions in the evidence of various witnesses – the men seen were wearing dark clothes, yet Mellor was seen to be wearing light clothes. The 'honest' witnesses swore to seeing four men together in the wood, yet Walker – on whose testimony the prosecution really did rely – swore they had not been all together. Some of these witnesses admitted they were a considerable distance away from the plantation. Parr changed his statement significantly on cross-examination, yet this fact does not seem to have been picked up by the defence. Not one witness positively identified any of the prisoners as being in the wood on the night of Horsfall's murder. If the defence witnesses who swore to seeing Mellor and Thorpe around Huddersfield at the pertinent time were lying, why were they not prosecuted for perjury?

These young workmen seem to have been using weapons which had only come into their possession on the day in question – with the possible exception of Thorpe who, it was suggested, frequently went armed. Pistols were not that accurate over a long distance, though it was suggested that Mellor had loaded his pistol with a large amount of shot. The Russian pistol could have had a barrel large enough to take a musket ball rather than the usual pistol shot, but that would not make it more accurate. It would probably be less accurate since the recoil from a gun loaded as has been suggested could cause the firer's arm to jerk and the shot to go wide of its mark. Yet all fired with remarkable accuracy on the day in question.

None of the evidence proves any incontrovertible link with the men convicted. Both prosecution and defence witnesses provide individual testimonies, which may or may not have been true. The trial took place more than six months after the event so memories may have been hazy. But that applies equally to prosecution and defence witnesses. The murder had a huge impact on the local society. If you were asked to remember an evening six months ago, it may prove difficult. But if it was linked to a major event? A great many would be able to say exactly what they were doing on the day Princess Diana died. Horsfall's murder would have had much the same impact on the local community.

It is equally possible that others were involved or even that someone simply took the opportunity to kill Horsfall knowing that the blame would fall on a group of young men who were known to be hotheads, were often heard shouting about what they would do and whom the authorities would easily believe to be the perpetrators.

The fact that this was a 'show trial' seems likely. The magistrate, Radcliffe of Milnsbridge House, had previously written to London requesting that the judge should be someone other than Bayley, who had presided over similar trials in Nottingham and was felt to be too lenient. Radcliffe was confident that they would hang the men, provided someone else had control of the court room. Discussions took place about where to hang the men – at the place where the murder occurred was suggested but was dismissed as being likely to cause a riot. Eventually it was agreed that they should be hanged in York and

Milnsbridge House where magistrate Joseph Radcliffe used to live. The Author

their bodies given to Leeds or York hospital surgeons for dissection. These discussions took place a week before the men came to trial!

Many prisoners waited some time between sentence and execution. Smith had been recommended for mercy but there was no time for any reprieve to arrive. Mellor, Thorpe and Smith were hanged just two days later.

Early in the morning, two troops of cavalry were drawn up in front of the execution 'drop' and all the avenues to the Castle were guarded by infantry. At 8.55 am, the prisoners 'came upon the fatal platform'. Mellor prayed aloud for ten minutes fervently and with devotion, 'confessing in general the greatness of his sins, but without any allusion to the crime for which he suffered'. Thorpe prayed but more quietly. Smith said little. The prisoners were then moved to the front of the platform, from where Mellor said, 'Some of my enemies may be here; if there be, I freely forgive them, and all the world, and I hope the world will forgive me.' Thorpe's comments were, 'I hope none of those who are now before me will come to this place.' Not only were the prisoners executed still chained in irons, but the authorities had altered the scaffold so that the whole of the body could be seen by the spectators, instead of just the head and feet as was usual. They were determined that the event would act as a lesson for all concerned. A great number of persons assembled for the occasion but 'the greatest silence reigned during the whole of this solemn and painful scene'. The *Leeds Mercury* ended with the comment:

> *And thus have perished in the very bloom of life, three young men; who, had they directed their talents to lawful pursuits, might have lived happy and respected. They were young men on whose countenances nature had not imprinted the features of assassins.*

The bodies were taken to the County Hospital, York for dissection and a strong military guard was needed for several nights to ensure the bodies were not removed.

CHAPTER 3

A Saturday Night Fight 1825

There is not a man able to fight me. I struck a man just now and he dare not strike me again.

Saturday night was the end of the working week and tra-ditionally a night when work was set aside and men went drinking. Saturday 20 August 1825 was no exception. James Dean had come over from Ashton-under-Lyne some time pre-viously to find work and had been working hard all week, labouring. He headed into Huddersfield ending up at Aspley, an area busy during the day with boats moving up and down the canal or loading and unloading on the wharves nearby. Serving the thirst of the working men was the Wharf Inn, run by Margaret Lockwood.

John Scott, a blacksmith, had come all the way down from Honley. At 11 pm he was leaving the Wharf Inn to go home when he saw James Dean and another man called Job Thornton coming past the door. Dean grabbed hold of Thornton's work apron and refused to let go,

The New Wharf Inn, Aspley. The Author

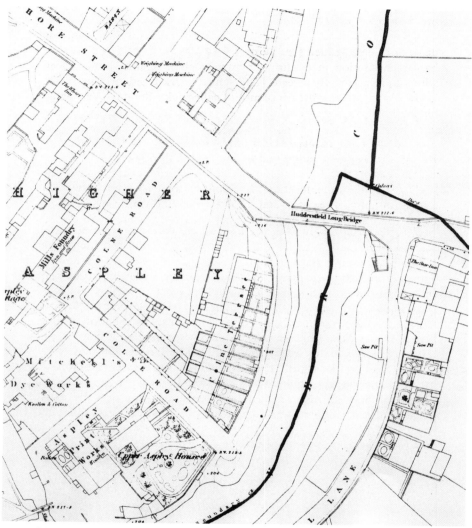

Map (1851) of Aspley area. Ordnance Survey

pulling the man back. Thornton tried to shake him off and said, 'If thou wants anything with me, come on.' They struggled violently and Job fell down. He got up again, but Dean struck him and he fell with the back of his head on the stone flags. Dean shouted, 'What's the matter with thee? I've not given thee enough. I will.'

At this point Scott hurried away and saw no more of them. Dean, with the cockiness of youth and drink, went on into the Wharf Inn, bragging to George Radley, saying, 'There is not a man able to fight me. I struck a man just now and he dare not strike me again.'

No wonder the man dared not strike him again. Thornton was lying dead on the roadside. The inquest, held on the following Tuesday, had no hesitation in confirming manslaughter against James Dean who was immediately arrested and sent to York Castle to await trial.

Mr Blackburn, for the prosecution, called John Scott who repeated his evidence, saying that he did not know how the quarrel began nor did he observe whether deceased fell over a stone. He was sure, however, that the prisoner struck him about the head or neck. William Broughton was also called and he confirmed the evidence.

Mr Thomas Wrigley, surgeon, resident at Huddersfield, opened the body and head of the deceased; he found on the back part of the head a great quantity of extravasated blood which had run into the spinal canal, this was the cause of death. There was a bruise on the forehead. Cross-examined, he said that the rupture of a blood vessel in the head might have been produced by a fall or a blow.

Mr Jones, defending the prisoner, called Obadiah Morland, a veterinary surgeon, resident of Ashton-under-Lyne who had known the prisoner from his youth. Morland stated that Dean was a waterman and had always been very peaceable and industrious and not at all disposed to be quarrelsome.

The jury found the prisoner guilty and he was sentenced to six months imprisonment and hard labour.

CHAPTER 4

An Unprovoked Attack 1825

Without warning, a group of men appeared...

In September 1825 James Wigglesworth, the coroner for Huddersfield, was called to view the body of Charles Read (or Reed), a joiner of Hillhouse. Read had been clinging to life for over six weeks but had finally succumbed to his wounds. Though a number of men seemed to have been involved in the affray only two were actually charged. The first, Thomas Brien (or Brian), an Irishman was committed to York Castle on 8 September, whilst John Glavan or Lavan was at liberty until 21 September.

The case was heard at the Spring Assizes in March the following year, Mr Blackburn and Mr Tudor prosecuting.

On Sunday 24 July Charles Read had been walking through an area known as the Beast Market, in company with some friends – Robert Driver, a mason, James Scatchard and John Kye. Without warning, a

Beast Market, Huddersfield. The Author

group of men appeared and attacked Reed. In the general melee, Driver floored three of them and the attackers were eventually driven off. Driver was able to identify Brien and Glavan, though neither Scatchard or Kye knew any of the attackers. Driver and his friends confirmed that they were sober and had offered no provocation. None knew of any previous quarrel.

The surgeon, Benjamin Hudson, described the bruises and wounds Read had received, agreeing that they were consistent with having been severely beaten. They were the cause of death, he said.

A verdict of manslaughter was given and both prisoners were given twelve months confinement with hard labour.

CHAPTER 5

A Most Barbarous and Brutal Murder
1830

If you knew what I was boon to do about it, you wouldn't rest, not by night or by day!

Rachel, the youngest child of Eli and Rachel Crosley, lived with her parents, and many of her thirteen siblings, in Thorncliffe Green, Kirkburton. Her father was a miner. Rachel was a very small child, and even at the age of twenty-two was always known as 'Little Rachel'.

When she was only seventeen, Rachel began seeing William Shaw, a young man just a few years older than herself. She expected marriage, and was promised it too, whereupon she gave in to his demands, resulting in an early pregnancy. William, however, reneged on his promise and their child, Harriet, was born illegitimate, on 26 August 1826 when Rachel was just eighteen. A bastardy order was sought and William was eventually ordered to pay four shillings (20p) a week for the child, though the payments were erratic and he was often in arrears with the money.

This was the time when the Poor Law had to provide the only form of 'social security' available and bastards were frowned upon. The church did not approve, local residents did not approve since the child would take its settlement from its place of birth and, in the event of the father not being known, or absconding, the parish was left to provide support.

The relationship continued, despite William persistently promising marriage but not actually getting to the church, until in 1829 it became obvious that Rachel was again pregnant. William came under increasing pressure from Rachel's family to marry her – pressure applied by others in the community too.

In March 1830 William visited the small beer shop run by Joe and Mary Butcher, almost opposite where Rachel lived. They began to

Looking across the fields towards the hamlet of Thorncliffe Green. The Author

tease him about the situation and asked him: 'What are you boon to do about it?'

William became more and more irritated by their remarks and eventually replied: 'If you knew what I was boon to do about it, you wouldn't rest, not by night or by day!'

Rachel's mother then arrived, asking William to go outside. 'Art thou for marrying yond lass or art thou not?' she asked him.

William replied that he had no objection, but that there was time yet. Rachel's mother disagreed and asked about banns.

'There's been a talk that you are spurred [dialect for reading the banns of marriage] somewhere,' she said, which William denied. 'Will you put the spurrings in, and where?' she asked.

William implied that he would do so on Sunday but was not sure where. Her mother informed him, 'We shall not turn her out, we shall take care of her a while.' 'You promise very fair, I'm sure,' he replied, agreeing eventually that he would see Rachel to tell her when the banns would be published.

The following evening, she sent Rachel out to fetch some coal, and later saw William outside their house.

On Monday 8 March, he was again at Mary Butcher's house when one of the village boys told him that Rachel was intending to apply to the parish for a 'warrant', meaning that William would yet again be hauled in front of the parish officials to account for his actions and to be ordered to pay for the second child. More teasing and ribald comments followed William as he stalked away in silence, brooding on his problems.

On Tuesday, Rachel sat down with her family to their supper. She ate nothing but just after 9 pm wrapped herself in her shawl, put on her cap and slipped outside. William was waiting for her and they stood together behind the house, talking for a few minutes before setting off to walk up the croft. She was never seen alive again.

Her parents became worried when she failed to return home by 10 pm but it was already too dark to do more than search in the immediate vicinity of the house. Next morning, work began early at the local pit, owned by Mr Green, just 200 yards from where the Crosley family lived. This was before much machinery was available so many mines were shallow. Deeper ones required men and children to be lowered down in a type of basket. The two boys who were first at work were duly lowered down, until the men on the surface heard them screaming out in terror. Quickly, they wound the basket back up and comforted the terrified boys. Eventually they were able to stammer out 'there was a dead man at the bottom of the pit, without any breeches'.

James Buckley, a collier, was then sent down and, finding the body of a young woman, called for assistance. With the help of another man, the body was brought to the surface where the extent of her shocking injuries could be seen. The skull was fractured. Some bones were broken, and there was extensive bruising. Her clothes were wrapped tightly around her thighs, which would have prevented her running away and much of her clothing was torn in a manner which suggested the damage had been done before she had been thrown down the pit. She was heavily pregnant.

A search was immediately made for footmarks in the area; those of a man and woman were found, coming along the croft, through two gaps at the corner of a field nearby and ending near to the mouth of the pit. Abraham Matthews and George Mountain discovered that one of the pair, the man's, were found to be very distinctive as some of the nails on the sole were missing.

By this time news of the discovery had reached the village and, in despair, when he learned that a warrant for his arrest had been issued, William surrendered himself to the constable. When his shoes were compared with the footprints, it was obvious that the pattern of

Map of Thorncliffe Green showing the pits in the area. Ordnance Survey

missing nails corresponded exactly. Unfortunately, after comparing the shoes with the imprints, the shoes were simply handed back to Shaw and were no longer available for the trial.

At the subsequent inquest, one of the doctors expressed his opinion that Rachel had been murdered before being thrown down the pit. William was heard to mutter, 'Nay she wur not, for she wur alive when she went into the pit mouth.'

He was committed to stand trial at the York Assizes.

Although he pleaded not guilty, Shaw offered no defence. Neighbours were called to confirm their relationship. Mary Haigh, next-door-neighbour to the Crosley family, confirmed that she had seen William and Rachel together on the Monday night, and again on the Tuesday, when she had at first thought it was her own daughter that the man was with. Rachel's mother had arrived around 10 pm searching for her daughter. It was Mary who had helped wash away the blood and lay out the poor girl when her body was finally recovered. She described the clothing as being torn and the top part of her skirt being wound tightly round her thighs. The jury suggested that the skirt had been tucked up to avoid the wet grass, but it was a clear, dry, moonlit night and Mary confirmed that the girl could not have walked with her skirt like that.

Benjamin Fitton, the local police constable, confirmed that Shaw had voluntarily given himself up. During the night they had conversed about the situation and he had said to the prisoner, 'Bill, if Joe Butcher's had not been such a bad house, and thee haunted it, this thing would not have happened.'

'It would not,' Shaw agreed, 'it will be a warning to others.'

After only a forty-five minute retirement the jury found him guilty. In silence the judge put on the black cap and told Shaw that he had

. . . been convicted of a most barbarous and brutal murder. There are instances in which, in the cases of persons who have suffered the last penalty of the law, there has been some reason for compassion for them,

Kirkburton Church. The Author

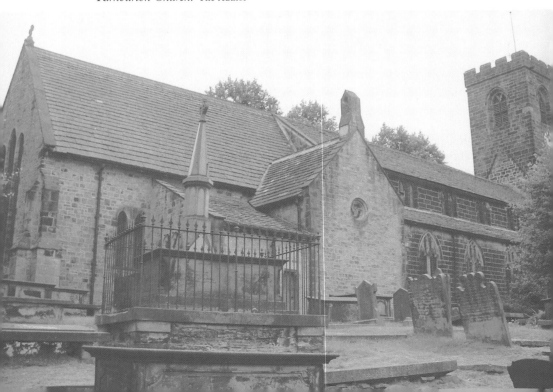

but your office is such, no one can have pity upon you. That unfortunate young woman, who was with child to you, and whom you had promised to become her husband, and ought to have been her protector, was enticed by you, to the place where you destroyed her in the most dreadful, barbarous and brutal manner.

Adjuring him to spend his last hours in prayer, the judge passed sentence of death, to 'be hung by the neck till you are dead, and your body be given to the surgeons for dissection; and may the Lord have mercy on your soul'.

Shaw seemed to be unaffected by this pronouncement. He was hanged on 5 April 1830, at York, on the 'new drop' behind the castle.

Rachel was buried in Kirkburton on 12 March 1830. On the same day, her little daughter, Harriet, was also finally baptised.

CHAPTER 6

A Stabbing in Kirkburton 1834

The carotid artery had been severed and the young man bled to death before morning.

On 26 November 1834 a group of young men decided to go on a 'pub-crawl' round some of the beer shops in Kirkburton, just a few miles outside Huddersfield. All went well until towards the end of the evening, as so often happens, a quarrel burst out amongst the group. Joseph Heeley became particularly belligerent, finally producing a knife and threatening to 'stab three or four of you before morning'.

The lads split up and rolled home, thinking nothing more of the incident. A short while later Charles Moseley, a weaver, was startled to find his front door burst open and Joseph Heeley outside, clutching at a neighbour's door for support. As Moseley reached his front door, the other door was opened by twenty-year-old James Lee, the eldest son of Kezia Hardcastle, who lived next door.

Heeley struck out, narrowly missing Lee, and then staggered off down the fold-yard, followed by both Lee and Moseley. As he reached the end of the yard he suddenly lashed out again at Lee, striking him in the neck. Heeley ran away, whilst Moseley cried out for help. Lee was taken to his mother's house.

Joseph Catterson, the surgeon, was immediately called, finding Lee covered in blood, with a two inch long wound below his ear. The carotid artery had been severed and the young man bled to death before morning.

The *Leeds Mercury* described it as 'one of the most horrible murders ever known to have taken place in Yorkshire'.

At the York Spring Assizes Messrs Greenwood and Wortley prosecuted, but Heeley had no defence counsel at all. Further witnesses were called who confirmed that Heeley had obtained the knife from one of the group, called Hill. Heeley then left the inn, along with a friend called Newsome. They were intending to go back to

Crown Court, York. The Author

Newsome's house to drink yet more liquor that they had purchased. On the way home they met another man when Joseph Heeley seized him by the coat and, looking into his face and said, 'If it had been the man I wanted, I would have run this knife into him.' He then let the man go and carried on walking into the village but when Heeley turned into the yard of one of the cottages, Newsome 'repeatedly desired him to go forward quietly and peaceably'. Heeley refused and Newsome left him there, whereupon 'The desperate man, who seemed determined to imbrue his hands in innocent blood, proceeded to knock at the door of the man named Moseley.'

The rest of the witnesses confirmed the earlier account of the stabbing but the newspaper continued:

> *What renders the circumstances still more disgusting, and as if to consummate this dreadful affair, Heeley proceeded to the house of Newsome, and took out the fatal knife for the purpose of cutting some bread. When the latter observed to him how the knife was bloody and he said 'Yes, this knife has been up to the haft in somebody's blood' and boasted of the horrible act he had committed.*

The prisoner's only defence was that the witnesses had sworn falsely.

It took the jury only ten minutes to agree on a verdict of guilty. The *Leeds Mercury* reported this fact and concluded:

> *The circumstances of this murder were fully detailed at the time of its occurrence and need not be repeated especially as they present only the*

disgusting features so common in such cases, of a man of low and dissi-
pated habits, under the madness of intoxication, striking about him
with wanton ferocity, and inflicting a fatal wound with his knife.

The paper went on to comment:

There is great cause for complaint of the want of sufficient activity in the
present constituted constabulary force in the neighbourhood where this
dreadful deed was perpetrated as it is dangerous for anyone to go out
after dark, owing to gangs of young men who prowl around the neigh-
bourhood for the express purpose of doing acts of mischief and annoying
those who may be passing by.

Heeley was hanged at York on 6 April 1835.

CHAPTER 7

Fratricide
1835

... in the midst of that horrible, mad drunkenness, you sent him, unprepared, into the presence of the tribunal of his God, to answer for his sins.

The Bray family ran a public house at Netherthong near Huddersfield during the early nineteenth century. The two brothers, Thomas and John, never really got on together.

On Christmas Day 1835, according to John Fearnley, who was drinking there at the time, Thomas was 'in liquor'; on being attacked by another drunken man called Armitage, he overturned a number of pints of ale. His brother commented that he could have managed Armitage without upsetting all the ale, to which Thomas retorted that he 'didn't care what damage he did in the house'.

This caused an argument to spring up between the brothers, resulting in Thomas being thrown out of the house and kept out for about an hour, during which time the two of them shouted and argued through the doors. Thomas threw out wild accusations, including suggesting that his brother had starved his wife to death. Finally he managed to get back into the house, smashing a load of glassware in the process. John grabbed a knife, exclaiming 'I'll either do him his job, or he shall do me mine'. Thomas, who was not wearing coat or waistcoat, rushed into the kitchen, hands up ready, shouting, 'Where is that devil!' The brothers threw themselves at each other and John stabbed Thomas in his left breast. Thomas fell to his knees and cried out 'Murder, he has a knife'. Their mother pleaded with others present to take the knife from John but no one succeeded in doing so. Thomas then tried again to get up but was tripped up by the prisoner. Again he tried to get up but this time his own father knocked him down. John lashed out again and again, inflicting three

One of the early police signs. The Author

deep cuts on his brother's thigh and stabbing him four times in the chest. One wound had entered between the eighth and ninth rib and the surgeon attributed death to this particular wound.

John was immediately arrested and later appeared at the Assizes in York on a charge of manslaughter. During the hearing, the Judge left the court whilst he consulted one of the other judges because he was concerned about the nature of the offence of which John Bray stood accused. He felt it should be murder rather than manslaughter, but he later returned and the case continued. Other witnesses came forward who suggested that it was Thomas who was the more violent, having earlier gone down into the cellar and knocked over barrels of beer, swearing that he would kill 'either his father or brother before midnight'. Thomas was a 'notorious fighter and nobody could stand against him'.

After describing these events, several witnesses appeared to give John a good character. When questioned, John said that he had been 'in bodily fear of this life' and pleaded that he acted in self-defence. The judge did not agree. In his summing up, which tends to direct the jury how to consider the case, he declared that the indictment was wrong and this 'was not a case of manslaughter, but of murder ... it was true that the prisoner might have received provocation but that was no justification for arming himself with a knife and going forth with a premeditated attempt to do some dreadful act'. The jury found Bray guilty.

The judge again consulted Mr Parke, another judge. On his return he spoke to the prisoner:

> *John Bray, this is the most painful case that it has been my unfortunate lot to try during the present Assizes and I am bound to say that at least one individual has suffered death for a less crime than yours; for I cannot entertain one moment's doubt that, according to the evidence, you have been found guilty of no less a crime than the murder of your own brother. Fortunate, indeed, is it for you that the indictment has put so merciful a construction upon your case – fortunate, indeed, is it for you, that you are not this day about to receive that sentence that you*

should die on Thursday, according to the crime which you have committed. In the midst of his undutiful conduct to his father – in the midst of that horrible, mad drunkenness, you sent him, unprepared, into the presence of the tribunal of his God, to answer for his sins. You have received a very good character, but that cannot weigh with me today. I am bound – the law is imperative upon me – that I should mark your offence with the severest sentence which is known to the crime of manslaughter, and that others may take warning by your fate. Think of the misery you have caused to your relations. Think of the horrid state of wickedness in which you sent your brother into the presence of his God and then think how fortune you must be, that for that immense amount of misery you are not about to receive the extreme sentence of the law. I have only to fulfil my duty by passing upon you the sentence of the court, which is, that you be transported beyond the seas for the term of your life, there to spend the remainder of your days in wretchedness and sorrow. Amongst the refuse of those wretches who have been expatriated from their native land; then, I hope, when you reflect upon your own miserable state, you may be constrained to say, in the language of the murderer of old, 'my punishment is too great for me to bear'.

However, John Bray was not transported overseas. Whilst waiting in York Castle to be taken, first to the hulks, and then to the transport ships, John died 'as is supposed of a broken heart'. It was reported at the same time:

The father of the two unfortunate young men is likewise in a very precarious state of health.

CHAPTER 8

A Violent Husband
1837

... she was in that state that ought to call forth all a husband's tenderness.

At the age of only twenty-three, Joseph Berry was lucky not to be hanged. On Saturday 29 July 1837, Joseph's wife, Mary, was sitting sewing buttons on her husband's clothes. They had been married barely two years, but for some reason never disclosed, an argument ensued, and Mary finally got up from her seat and went out, stopping to rest at the top of the steps nearby. Joseph followed her out, still arguing. In a fit of temper, Joseph knocked her to the ground, kicking her again and again in the back and side. His anger spent, he returned inside the house and left Mary lying there. She was heavily pregnant with their first child.

Before any of their neighbours could come to her aid, she had died from the effects of the beating she had received.

An inquest was quickly arranged, held in the Red Lion Inn, Lockwood before Mr Stocks. It did not take the jury long to bring in

The Red Lion Inn, Lockwood. The Author

Holy Trinity Church, South Crosland. The Author

a verdict of manslaughter against Joseph Berry, who was then committed to York Castle to await his trial at the next assizes.

He had quite a long wait in the Castle prison. It was not until March the following year that the case finally came before Justice Coleridge. Berry pleaded guilty. Although Mr Bliss, in his defence, called several witnesses who, according to contemporary reports, 'gave the prisoner a good character for humanity previous to committing the offence of which he pleaded guilty and who also stated that he displayed great contrition for it'. The judge was not impressed. In passing sentence, the judge said, 'there was no proof that he [Berry] entertained any preconceived malice against her [his wife]', otherwise he would probably have faced a charge of murder. Judge Coleridge went on to say that he had

> ... *never known an instance of passion carried to such an extent for he had followed his wife and repeatedly kicked her upon the body, not only when she was flying from him, but when she was in that state that ought to call forth all a husband's tenderness and he was sorry to say that such cases were of too frequent occurrence in this Riding of which the calendar of these assizes afforded too abundant evidences and therefore he should be wanting in his duty if he did not pass a severe sentence in the present circumstances.*

The prisoner was then sentenced to be transported for the rest of his natural life. This proved to be shorter than he possibly expected. Joseph Berry was taken to the hulk *Fortitude* in Chatham where he stayed for a further seven months before finally sailing in October 1838 on the transport ship, *Theresa*. He died just four years later, in New South Wales.

Mary Berry was buried in Holy Trinity church, South Crosland, on 1 August 1837, aged just twenty-five.

CHAPTER 9

A Complete Mystery
1837

... heard screams there about 2 am but did nothing.

On 12 August 1837 considerable alarm was raised in Huddersfield by the discovery of a body of a woman in New Street. It was close to the steps of a factory owned by M J Schofield. The body was taken to the Commercial Inn opposite and on examination proved to be that of Mrs Sunderland, wife of John Sunderland, a cooper, of King Street, Huddersfield. It appeared that she had left home about 9.30 pm the previous evening to look for her husband who, she imagined, would stop out late because there were three different meetings that evening that he had intended to go to.

Map (1851) showing the site of the Commercial Inn, Huddersfield. Ordnance Survey

Present day Commercial Hotel, New Street, Huddersfield. The Author

However, he returned home about 11 pm. He was told his wife had gone to seek him, but apparently went off to bed without waiting up for her.

It was said that some women who lived in the yard heard screams there about 2 am but did nothing. No one knew where she went during the evening or if she met up with friends – or anyone else. When discovered, her bonnet was found tied up and lying beside her. No marks of violence appeared on her, except a slight bruise above one eye that may have been caused by a fall.

Mrs Sunderland was 'a most respectable woman and of strictly sober habits [and] intoxication is an idea totally out of the question'. It was thought that she might have been with someone and afterwards perhaps had a fit and that those persons whoever they were, were afraid of being blamed so removed her to the spot where she was found.

This idea seemed corroborated by the appearance of her heels and feet, which were scuffed as if the body had been dragged along – but how she actually came there or who she had been with, remained a mystery. It was evident she could not have had a fit there, or her bonnet would not have been tied up and laid beside her and the place being very dark, she would not have gone there on her own account.

A post-mortem examination was made on Saturday night but no internal appearances of violence were found. When the body was discovered, one arm was bent across her stomach; the other was straight by her side. It does not appear that robbery was the motive, which renders the whole case more mysterious.

On the Monday, an inquest was held before M Stocks Esq and a 'respectable jury'. The evidence produced threw no further light on the mysterious affair. The jury therefore brought in a verdict of 'found dead' thus leaving the matter open for future investigation.

No answer was ever found to this mysterious death.

CHAPTER 10

Horrible Murder of the Head Police Officer 1840

He sprang forward at the same instance and plunged a pruning knife into his body.

We have this week to record one of the most appalling cases of savage brutality and murder which the annals of crime can furnish. The horrible scene took place last Tuesday in Huddersfield, which we will give in the language of our correspondent, who was an eyewitness of most of the dreadful particulars.

Last Tuesday, after tea, I paid one of my usual visits to our beautiful public Exhibition and while in conversation with a friend, I heard the cry of 'murder' and rushed out of the back door, close to which stands our prison and the prison-house. The crowd around soon told me in what course to direct my steps, and I immediately entered the prison house. The first object that struck my attention was Danson, one of our police officers, seated in a chair, literally stifled with the blood which he was stroking from his head and neck and which was streaming from other parts of his body. All was consternation and horror. The cries of Mrs Duke and other females that her husband was murdered, induced me to hasten into the prison yard, there to witness a scene that beggars description. Blood was so largely scattered in every direction, that the place resembled a slaughter house. There I found Duke, our head police officer, weltering in his blood, pale with exhaustion and Mr Wrigley, surgeon, on his knees vainly attempting to stop the bleeding. I rushed

Headlines from the Leeds Mercury. Author's collection

HORRIBLE MURDER
OF THE
HEAD POLICE OFFICER OF HUDDERSFIELD.

back to the front door – sent for all the surgical assistance to be found and then returned to the scene of horror to hear the piteous request of the dying officer 'Don't remove me, Doctor, don't be so cruel – let me die here!' were nearly his last words.

[Huddersfield & Holmfirth Examiner]

The man went on to investigate what had happened. The name of the perpetrator of the 'horrible deed' caused some confusion in spelling and probably pronunciation too. Alexander McLaughlan (or M'Giachan) Smith had come down from Scotland, seeking work. He had found lodgings in Elland where, it was said he 'has been an object of dread from his violence'. This day he had come into Huddersfield and, as a gardener himself, soon began looking at the plants for sale. He thought he had been offered a bargain. On being told that the price of a plant was 'eighteen pence', Smith asked, 'Will you take two pence?' In banter, the owner said, 'Yes,' whereupon Smith threw down two pence, seized the plant and walked off with it. The florist pursued him, but Smith refused to give the plant up. In the ensuing argument, Constable Danson arrived, suggesting that the matter should be laid before the magistrates who were in session nearby. However, it being 4 pm it was soon found that the session had ended and Danson then tried to take Smith to the police cells, where:

Being slightly affected with liquor, he resisted, and became very rough, especially when taken into the prison yard, where he made an attempt to injure Duke with a pruning knife, which was taken from him and a leg and a wrist chain were put on him and he was locked up.

Smith was searched and a small box, a pocket book, two pencils and a clasp knife were removed. The search proved to be not careful enough.

At about 6 pm Duke, Danson and Dalton, the three Huddersfield police officers, agreed to meet and search and secure him more closely. The lock-up was situated behind Duke's house and the actual access to it was through the house. Duke opened the door of his cell and asked what he meant by his conduct, since the man was still shouting and swearing at the top of his voice.

'What's all this noise about?' Duke said.

'I'll let you see' replied Smith 'you damned . . .'

He sprang forward at the same instance and plunged a pruning knife into Duke's body. The attack being so sudden and Duke taken by surprise he had no chance to avoid the blow. He stepped back and tried to get away, but Smith pursued and cut at him lashing upwards with the knife. The prisoner, though chained, had not been fastened

ALEXANDER MACLAUGHLAN SMITH.
THE MURDERER

Artist's impression of Smith from the Leeds Mercury. Author's collection

to the wall. Very soon Duke fell and Danson got hold of him. Smith immediately assaulted Danson in the same 'savage manner' and in an incredibly short time inflicted nine severe wounds on his head, body and thighs. All the policemen were unarmed with the exception of Dalton and he had only his wooden truncheon. When the fracas commenced he drew it out of his pocket but never had opportunity of using it. He ran in an opposite direction to the others in order to meet the three half way round the prison; by that time, Duke was laid prostrate, and Danson was wrestling with the prisoner and bleeding. Dalton knocked the knife out of Smith's hand and, with the assistance of the many men who had by this time run into the yard, managed to secure him. The prisoner displayed no remorse, but said to Dalton:

Damn you, you with the red stick, I'll do for you too.

Mr Wrigley, surgeon, soon arrived and attended first to Duke. He found him:

. . . deluged in his own blood, a frightful wound within the thigh divided the femoral artery and he was evidently sinking fast; no skill could save him, he was dead in fifteen or twenty minutes.

The post-mortem eventually found that Duke had five gashes: one to the left groin, six inches long and two inches deep; one to the right hip, nine inches long; one which divided the right arm muscles; one on the right thigh eight inches long and one which divided the femoral artery.

Danson was sent to the infirmary, where he remained for over a month and it was feared that he too would die from his wounds, but fortunately he survived:

The dreadful news of the murder spread rapidly and crowds assembled around the prison. The wretched prisoner in his frenzy rejoiced in his success and regretted he had not killed more. I remonstrated with him but was only threatened with the same fate could he reach me. The wretch was shortly after doubly pinioned and left for the night. The

Original infirmary buildings, now part of Huddersfield Technical College. The Author

> *morning came and I was kindly permitted to see the prisoner, whose mind still remained callous, without a symptom of remorse or of the slightest regret, save that he had hurt his own fingers.*

On Wednesday, an inquest was held at the George Inn, before Thomas Dyson, Esq, and a jury. The whole town seemed to have turned out to see the event and when the prisoner was brought in an open carriage, in bloodstained clothes, unwashed hands and an 'air of savage indifference nay, even a smile on his cognisance the expression of indignation was fearful'. The evidence was listened to carefully but before the jury gave their verdict the coroner asked the prisoner if he had any questions to ask:

> *. . . when with fiendish look and sarcastic sneer he replied 'Me ask any questions? Aren't you satisfied with what you've got? Then be doing.'*

The jury, without withdrawing to consider further, unanimously agreed a verdict of wilful murder. Shortly after the prisoner was committed and driven off to York Castle to take his trial at the next Summer Assizes:

> *. . . amidst a dense crowd whose suppressed indignation under the horrid exciting circumstances of this tragic scene does them great credit.*

The reports give Smith's description as being occasionally employed on the Manchester and Leeds Railway, dressed in a 'new suit of fustian, literally covered with blood, double breasted blue waistcoat and without neckerchief'. Crucially,

On the prisoner's coat were many marks of the blood of his victim, particularly on the right side just over the pocket.

Smith was said to be about thirty-four years of age, with sandy hair and whiskers, high cheek bones; about five feet seven inches high, strongly built and very broad in the chest; with 'a peculiarly savage aspect' and 'small fiendish eyes'. He was a native of Scotland, having a wife and two children at Stirling in 'indifferent circumstances'. During the whole of the inquest he showed the utmost callousness and indifference, even scorn. The knife used was a strong-made pruning knife, with a sturdy, hooked blade of about three and a half inches in length. Apparently, there was no remorse:

From the first to last he remained unmoved. The prisoner expressed his gratification of the result of his brutality and said he could wish to serve thirty more the same way.

On his road to York he was the same, and actually said that he thought no more of killing men that acted to him as the police had done than of killing bullocks.

The journey to York was made via Leeds, where the party arrived about 3.30 pm on Wednesday afternoon. He was taken in a post chaise, doubled ironed and in the custody of four police officers. Being too late for the 3 pm train the prisoner was taken to the gaol for safe custody and remained till 5.30 pm. He got out of the chaise and walked across the yard 'with the greatest possible composure and cast a ferocious glance at the persons who had surrounded the palisades inclosing the building'. Inside, he sat down on a bench till the gaoler came to place him in a cell. During those few minutes he remained quiet, but no sooner did the gaoler appear and start trying to lock him up, than:

. . . the cold-blooded monster again displayed his ferocity and although as before mentioned doubly ironed, he contrived to kick one of the Huddersfield officers in a most violent manner on the right leg. It is utterly impossible to describe the scene. The wretch talked of nothing but blood and if by any means he could have released himself from his irons and become armed with a knife or other deadly weapon, there is no doubt that a repetition of the Huddersfield tragedy would have followed.

About 5.30 pm he was taken to the railway station. By this time he was quiet and he was safely lodged in York Castle in the evening. It was said that 'His appearance whilst being conveyed through the streets of the city excited much horror'. On arrival in York he spoke to Mr Barker and Mr Noble, the castle governors, complaining that he had been 'ill used'.

On Tuesday 21 July 1840, before Mr Baron Rolfe, Alexander M'Glachan Smith was charged with having on the 29 April, at Huddersfield, killed by cutting and stabbing, William Duke of the police.

Mr Baines and Mr Lister were for the prosecution. Mr Wortley defended the prisoner.

Witnesses called included: John Danson, who had been a police officer for three years, William Leonard who was the market gardener; Francis Dalton, police officer; Thomas Wrigley, surgeon at Huddersfield (who confirmed that the prisoner was of sound mind and capable of knowing right from wrong); Thomas Shepherd, a reed maker and customer at the gardener's stall; and Godfrey Mann, working for Mr Jennings, railway contractor, who had worked with prisoner and employed him as a gardener. The latter considered him to be a good gardener and did not consider him to be insane. William Greenwood, surgeon at Huddersfield infirmary, also confirmed the prisoner was 'of sound mind'. Others who felt the prisoner was perfectly aware of what he was doing included Mr Champney, surgeon of York Castle and William Anderson, his partner; John Noble, Governor of the Castle; John Abbey, turnkey at the Castle and Mr Baxter Barber Under Governor of the Castle.

However, Thomas Noble, from Elland, said the prisoner lodged with him. He had seen him subject to fits, often two or three in quick succession, of such severity that he was often not able to work because of them. In those days epilepsy was seen as a form of insanity, violence alternating with bouts of tranquillity. Mr Wortley, for the defence, argued that he should never have been arrested in the first place and that the attack had happened in a passion and the charge should therefore have been manslaughter, not murder. As he suffered epilepsy, he was therefore insane anyway, thus he had suffered 'a paroxysm of frenzy in which he was incapable of distinguishing right from wrong'.

William Brook, surgeon, of Stainland, had bled the prisoner because of fits, but he did not feel that they confirmed insanity.

Walter Smith, chemist and druggist at Elland, frequently served the prisoner medicines and did feel the man was insane, whilst John Worth, a labourer from Elland, said that the prisoner had lodged with him on Saturday before murder, when he had been raving and getting violent and Caleb Williams, the general manager of Friends' Retreat in York had examined the prisoner and stated that his 'intellect

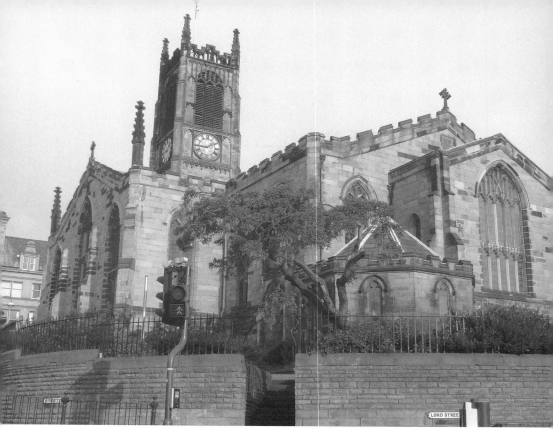

Huddersfield Parish Church as it is today. The Author

was impaired and his moral sense weakened by the disease'. He was labouring under delusions as to alleged recriminations from Jesus Christ.

After one hour's deliberations the jury acquitted Smith on the grounds of insanity and the judge ordered him to be confined in the Castle during Her Majesty's Pleasure.

The funeral of William Duke took place at the parish church. He had come from Hull in about 1832 to be chief policeman in Huddersfield. Various members of his family and many police officers from towns and villages in the area also attended. A massive gathering of people followed the corpse of the murdered man to the grave. He had been known as an 'amiable person' and 'his uniform kindness to all classes of the inhabitants and the conscientious and efficient manner in which he discharged the duties of his office' created even more grief than usual.

A subscription for Mrs Duke, the widow of the police officer, was set up. She had witnessed the murder of her husband but was described as 'in a dreadful state of mind but as well as can be expected'.

CHAPTER 11

Child Murder
1851

One baby that had been born recently in the workhouse had just been taken home by his mother.

Nowadays, a simple DNA test can establish relationships. In earlier times it was much more difficult to be sure of identity, but when Edward Holmes pulled a baby's body out of the mill goit, the police were certain they knew who was the mother.

Edward Holmes, of Kilner Bank, Dalton was a stone-dresser working for Varley and Co at Shorefoot mill. On Thursday morning 25 August 1851 he found a child in the goit of Shorefoot mill dam. At first he thought that the object was a dog but on turning it over with a rake he saw the child's face. He let it go gently back into the water and called for the assistance of two other men, one of whom, Arthur Derbyshire, had to go to Commercial Street that morning so he was told to call at the police office and let them know what had been found. Superintendent Thomas arrived later that morning and took charge of the body.

The child had on a cap, a printed dress, binder, chemise and cloth marked 'Huddersfield Union No 11'. Superintendent Thomas and Sergeant William Townend set off for Kirkheaton workhouse. Charlotte Mottershead, the matron of the workhouse, confirmed that the clothes did belong to Kirkheaton. One baby that had been born recently in the workhouse had just been taken home by his mother.

An inquest on the body was held on Saturday afternoon at the Bull and Mouth Inn, Victoria Street near the Guildhall 'before George Dyson and the following respectable jury: John Firth, foreman, Thomas Marshall, Jabez Brook, Robert Spivey, Abram Walker, Jonas Walker, Benjamin Gibson, George Starkey, George Mitchell, Joseph Person, John Labrey, and James Heron'.

The jury were sworn in and viewed the body of the child, which was at the police office. The first witness called to give evidence was

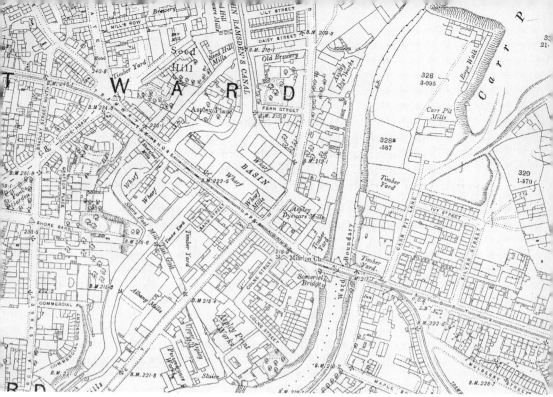

Map (1893) of Shorefoot showing the Mill Goit. Ordnance Survey

Charlotte Mottershead, aged fifty, wife of John Mottershead. She was the matron of Kirkheaton workhouse and confirmed that Frances Cooke had been in the workhouse something less than four months. Her evidence was reported as follows:

> I do not know Charles Cooke but that was the name she gave. Five weeks past last Thursday on 22 August the prisoner was delivered of a male child, as fine a child as they had ever had in the workhouse. There was nothing the matter with the child whilst it was there. It was registered by the name of John Herbert Cooke. At first it was only registered Herbert Cooke but the prisoner said her sister had complained that she did not call it John and I said she might put John to it. She left the workhouse with the child four weeks after it was born. I saw them to the bottom of the lane when they went out. She asked to lend her a suit of clothes for she had none with her and should return them when she got to her mother's. She asked me in the morning to let her go to Huddersfield as she wanted to see Mr Wheatley and she could get admitted into the Board Room on Friday. I told her if she would stop until the afternoon one of the men was going and he would carry her the bigger child.

The clothes that were taken off the child when it was found were then shown to Mrs Mottershead and she thought they belonged to the workhouse; some were marked with the letter of the Union. The shift did not belong to the workhouse. She confirmed that 'I never saw her [Frances] misbehave to the child; she behaved well and in a kind manner to it. I never saw anything to the contrary.'

Next came George Heaton. He had been an agricultural labourer and stated that he had been living in Kirkheaton workhouse between three and four years. He continued:

I knew Frances Cooke when she came to lie in. I left on the day she left, it is a week since last Thursday, to come to Huddersfield with her. Mrs Mottershead said it was our best way on by the canal side. I hugged the big child. When we got to the cut bridge at the bottom of Huddersfield she [Frances] said she could do herself. I then stopped to see how she

Map (1854) showing the site of Kirkheaton workhouse. Ordnance Survey

managed and watched her on the road to Lockwood as far as the lime
kilns. She was walking steadily on. We left the workhouse about 3 pm
and got to the cut bridge about 4.30 pm. The distance is about three
miles. I know nothing more.

The canal path follows a lonely route, with no houses nearby. Frances
was holding the elder boy, carrying a basket as well as the baby and
was trying to suckle the baby as she walked.

Frances' sister, Emma Hopkinson, wife of John Hopkinson, of
Manchester Road, Huddersfield said she did not see her sister from
the time of her going to the workhouse in Kirkheaton until her return
on Thursday evening. She told the court:

After tea between 5 and 6 pm, I met the prisoner near the Albion Hotel
at the top of Chapel Hill, when she had her little boy who is about two
years of age with her and a basket on her arm. I did not see the contents
of the basket. I said, 'where's your child?' prisoner said 'It's dead and
buried'. She began to fret and I left her immediately, saying, 'I cannot
hear you now but I will come down to my mother's'. I went down that
night and asked again about the child, when she told me the child died
on Monday previous and was buried on Wednesday. I asked where it
had been buried and she said at Kirkheaton church. I have seen my
sister this morning in the lock-up but nothing there passed relative to
the child. The basket she had on her arm was 12 by 6 inches. It was her
own basket and would have been taken with her when she went to
Kirkheaton.

Superintendent Thomas said he went to Shorefoot mill dam and saw
the child's body. He sent for a hamper to put it in and took it to the
station house before taking the clothes to Kirkheaton workhouse for
identification. He then went to the house of the prisoner's mother,
Mrs Hiley, in Dale Street. The prisoner was there. When they opened
the door, he asked Frances if she had some clothes belonging to
Kirkheaton 'poor house'. She said she had, that they were made up in
a bundle and that George Heaton should have called at the Board
Room for them. She produced the bundle.

He then asked 'Have you got a child?' to which she replied 'My
child is dead' and told him it was buried in Kirkheaton poor house.
On being asked from whom she got the certificate to register the child
she said, 'Mr Dyson registered it.'

Superintendent Thomas then enquired what she was doing with
the bundle if she had no child and Frances told him that a woman at
Moldgreen had given them to her to send to Kirkheaton poorhouse.
She said that her child had died after two days sickness. When told

Kirkheaton Church. The Author

that she must go with the police to this woman at Moldgreen and the prisoner replied that she did not know her. Frances was then taken to the county lock-up and told the charge against her. She said George Heaton helped her to carry the children to Huddersfield. Thomas commented:

> ... *she added – and I did not ask her any question – 'I did not do it myself; I hope you will be as merciful to me as you can'.*

Sergeant William Townend of the Huddersfield police had accompanied Mr Thomas to the Huddersfield and Kirkheaton poor houses and also to the house of the prisoner's mother in Dale Street. He was able to corroborate the conversations held but also added that when asked how she got her children down from Kirkheaton, the prisoner had answered, 'George Heaton helped me to carry them to Green Cross. Sometimes he carried the elder and sometimes the younger one.' When asked, 'But I thought you buried the younger one at Kirkheaton?' she had said, 'I beg you will not mention it; I did not do it myself, I hope you will be as merciful to me as you can.'

However, when Mrs Mottershead (the workhouse matron) was recalled she could not identify the child nor say whether the child at the police office was Frances Cooke's child or not, but confirmed that the printed night gown, linsey woolsey barrow and the half of a hand-kerchief produced by Mr Thomas as the contents of the bundle delivered up by the prisoner, were the same the child had on when it left the workhouse. The nightgown in which the child was found was that used by the prisoner's oldest boy while in the house.

William James Clarke, surgeon, explained that he had examined the body of the child on the Thursday evening and also on the Friday morning. He said:

The face was beginning to decompose. The remaining part of the body was quite fresh. On the left side there was a severe bruise . . . there was no other mark of violence. On opening the body I examined the head; the brain was found healthy but congested on the face; the lungs were healthy and slightly congested; the heart was perfectly healthy; the right side distended with fluid blood, the left empty; the stomach was healthy and contained a little half digested food, apparently milk. All the other vessels were perfectly healthy and nothing peculiar in appearance. It was a fine plump fat child about twenty-two inches long and had the appearance of being six or seven weeks old. The body was a little swollen with being in the water, which would give the appearance of being older that it really was. I suppose it must have been in the water seven or eight days. My belief is that the deceased died from drowning; my opinion is grounded upon the absence of all disease and from the state of the brain, the lungs and heart. There are appearances in bodies when drowned that are absent here but still I believe drowning to be the cause of death.

Mr Barker asked, 'Might the wound arise from the child going forcibly against a hard substance?'

'Undoubtedly so,' was the reply from the surgeon.

'Is the wound of any consequence?'

'There is nothing in the child to show that the wound was the cause of death or to contradict the supposition of accidental drowning.'

'Was the child so much decomposed as to render it difficult to identify the child?'

'The face of the child was livid and bloated. The tongue swollen and protruded. It could not have been identified without difficulty.'

'Do you think that it would be safe for anyone to identify it as a particular child?'

'When I first saw the child, no one, from the features, could say that it was any particular child.'

Mrs Mottershead was again questioned by Mr Barker, particularly about the clothes the baby was wearing. She agreed that she couldn't tell how long before the Thursday the items marked '11' had been taken away from the workhouse:

> *I did not see the child dressed on that day. The double might have been taken away before Frances left, the children had only part of a bed tick on, neither of them had anything belonging to the workhouse to my knowledge. The things they had worn were left all right. I did not see them dressed.*

When asked by one of the jury she stated that she never saw anything in Frances Cooke like insanity, that she was rather a reserved character. When she left she had thanked the matron for her kindness who had replied that she had done nothing more than her duty.

George Heaton was also recalled to confirm that the dress was not changed after leaving the workhouse.

Once again, Edward Holmes was questioned about the goit of Shorefoot mill dam, explaining that it was connected with the cut and the stream had drawn the child against the grate where he had found it.

Next, Mary Jane Heaton, daughter of Superintendent Heaton, keeper of the county lock-up, was questioned. She confirmed that Frances Cooke had been in the lock-up since the previous Friday, having been brought in about 5 pm:

> *I went in several times to see her. The first time I went to see her I asked her what she was brought for and she said she did not know herself. I went in between eight and nine o'clock in the evening; she was wringing her hands and seemed in great trouble. I asked her what she had been thinking about to do such a thing. She replied 'I do not know. I must have been deprived of my senses to do such a thing. I thought of going in myself and taking this in too – pointing to the child that was then asleep on the bed.'*
>
> *I asked her if she had not been uneasy since she did it and she said 'Yes I have been so unhappy I have thought many a time of going and drowning myself.' She said many times, 'I am a guilty woman, shall ever I be forgiven.' That was the whole of the conversation I had with her about the child at that time.*

She agreed that the woman had seemed quite sane, and when asked by the jury, stated:

> *We are in the habit of asking questions to parties brought to the lock-up without giving them warning that it will be used against them. The reason I went in so often was my father desired me to go in and see her from fear she should injure herself or her child.*

After the depositions had been signed the coroner said to the jury:

Gentlemen, it is for you to consider the evidence. The first point I wish to draw your attention to is, are you quite satisfied upon what you have heard at this inquest that the child which is found, is the child of Frances Cooke? It is necessary that the body before you should be identified. If you are not satisfied from the appearance of the child when it was found you must be quite satisfied from other circumstances that it is the body of John Herbert Cooke. The only thing that appears to identify it are the clothes it had on when found, which were not those it had on when it left the workhouse. If you are not satisfied as to the identity of the child you will of course return a verdict of found drowned.

The jury then retired for a few minutes and returned with the following verdict:

We are unanimously of opinion that there is not sufficient evidence to confirm the identity of the child to be the child of Frances Cooke, consequently we return of verdict of found drowned.

However, the case went forward to the Assizes and in December Frances Cooke appeared before the judge. The only additional evidence seems to have been that of a messenger who had been sent from the workhouse to ask for the clothes back. Mrs Mottishead seems to have forgotten this and the fact that Frances apparently told him that the baby was at her mother's.

Frances had also been before the Board of Governors to ask for help since her husband, Charles who had previously worked as a waiter at the George Hotel, had deserted her. They agreed to allow her four shillings (20p), and she was heard to comment 'Is that all for three of us?'

The defence took the line that there was no definite evidence that the baby was actually her baby, but if it was then the death was an accident and she had let the baby fall in the canal due to her weakened state.

Something about Frances must have touched the jury because they agreed with the defence and pronounced her not guilty.

This raises a number of questions. Why was the surgeon so sure the child had drowned, when he admitted himself that 'There are appearances in bodies when drowned that are absent here'? The matron's evidence seemed to change. She first stated that 'she saw them to the bottom of the lane when they went out' and that she had lent them some clothes. Yet when she was recalled she stated, 'I did not see the child dressed on that day.' She may not have been present when the child was being dressed, but she apparently saw them off the

Shorefoot, looking towards the site of the mill with its water supply. The Author

premises and would have noticed some of the clothes, and the cap on the baby. She also failed to mention the messenger sent to fetch back the clothes.

The judge was very careful to draw the jury's attention to the identity of the baby, stating that the clothes giving identification were 'not the clothes it had on' when it left the workhouse, yet no one was really sure what clothes it was wearing when it was taken from the workhouse.

Perhaps most important of all, if the child had died in Kirkheaton, someone must have buried it. Why were no witnesses called to confirm whether this had or had not taken place? If Frances was telling the truth it was a simple matter to confirm that her child had died previously. If it had not, where was it? Was it in fact the poor little bundle that had been mistaken at first for a dog when it had been dragged from the canal? We shall never know for certain.

CHAPTER 12

Occupational Hazard 1851

Stand every man and fire, there's only eight of them.

In September 1851 the police court heard a case of 'trespassing in pursuit of game', an occupation which was very much frowned upon by the magistrates – many of whom either owned the land and game rights, or were close friends of those who did.

Samuel Holt, William Bardsley, Henry Greenwood, Henry Wild were charged with trespassing in company with five other persons 'not yet in custody' on land owned by Mr John Dowse, a corn miller and merchant of Hey Green in Marsden, 'for the purpose of searching for game on 29 August thereby subjecting themselves to a penalty of £5 each'.

William Schofield, William Hulhouse and John Whitehead, gamekeepers, gave evidence in support the charge. Greenwood had to be discharged as his identity was not so clearly established as that of the rest, but the other defendants were fined £1 plus expenses of £1 16s 6d (£1.79) each or in default of payment, be committed to Wakefield prison for two months.

However, things did not finish there. A few weeks previously, another case had been heard, during which 'some person' had fired a shot at the gamekeepers. At the conclusion of the later case, the police asked for a remand of Samuel Holt who had been identified by Joseph Bulmer, a gamekeeper, as the person who fired the loaded gun. Holt, on hearing this appeared much surprised and offered bail for his appearance; the bench however refused to accept it and consequently he was remanded until Tuesday, when he was charged with firing a loaded gun at Joseph Bulmar at Marsden on the 12 August 1851. Mr Clough appeared for the prosecution and Mr Cobbett of Manchester was present on behalf of the prisoner.

Joseph Bulmar said he was a labourer, working for Mr Dowse of Marsden:

Across the moors above Marsden and Outlane. The Author

On the morning of the 12 August, we started from Marsden about 1.30 am to go to the moors, and arrived there about 3 am. I went as a watcher for Mr Dowse; there were eighteen of us. We lay down about 200 yards off one another until 4 am, when we heard some shouting and whistling; we then ran in the direction where it was and got among some poachers. The other nine of our party had run away when we got to the poachers, and as we were going across we heard guns fired at them. There were several guns fired. We came up to the poachers when they were in pursuit of the other nine men. When the poachers saw us they retreated and ran away about thirty yards. I was the first man in our lot and the closest to them. I ran one person across a 'gruff' as they call it. Samuel Holt stood on the other side, opposite me. He said, 'Stand every man and fire, there's only eight of them.' He then fired his barrel off and presented the gun in the direction where I was. The shot came rushing about my heels and among the heath. I turned round to run then, as the rest of my party did not come up. When I had run a few yards he said 'Come out of them bottoms, chaps and fire, there's no man can tell how many there is of them.' We then got our lot together, the whole eighteen, and went up to them and they ran away over the boundaries.

Bulmar was in no doubt about the prisoner being the man that fired the gun or of its being loaded.

Cross-examined by Mr Cobbett, he described in more detail where they had been:

> *We went between 200 and 220 yards along the road to the place where we divided. We were 200 yards wide of them and 100 yards off the road, on the road to Oldham. This was on the 'Hassocks' in the Marsden boundary about half a mile. It is broken-up land. We went from the highway a little first to the left and then to the right, but leaving the highway all the time. When we first saw the poachers, they were in pursuit of the rest of our men. We heard four or five shots. I think the grouse were in danger from these men. They were running towards the 'gruff' where our men turned up. I was first of our party; the rest might be twenty or thirty yards behind me. Henry Berry was next to me, and the rest were squandered about, there were five or six of them within sixty yards of me but I cannot say exactly. There were twenty-five or thirty of the poachers and they were squandered also. We could not see the other nine of our men; the poachers had run them down and when the poachers saw us they retreated. Holt was the first man but one chasing the nine watchers. It was the first man that had a gun. I saw Holt clearly; he stood six yards from me when he fired, there was a 'gruff' between us. I felt the shot all about my legs. I don't know whether I was hit or not. I don't know on which side the shot came. There was a man down at the bottom of the 'gruff' who had run in, there was nothing else between us. I am sure Holt was the man who fired. I have seen him before, but did not know his name till Saturday last.*

The prosecutor, Mr Clough, wanted to clarify when Bulmar had made the charge:

> *The first time I made a charge against him was on Saturday last. I got his name by hearing others call him Holt. I picked him out amongst four men, as the man I saw fire the gun. I was not a witness in the other cases but came to Huddersfield purposely to make a charge against the prisoner. No one gave me a description of him.*

Henry Berry, on being sworn, confirmed that he lived at Marsden, working as a gamekeeper for Dowse. The shot had scattered on the ground and even touched his coat lapels. Mr Cobbett asked how far away he was when the shooting was taking place:

> *I was thirty or forty yards from the 'gruff' when the shot was fired. I was running after them when they crossed the 'gruff'.*

Berry's evidence was somewhat contradictory at this point:

I did not see them cross the 'gruff'. I did see them cross the 'gruff'; about eleven or twelve crossed at the same time. I did not see the man that fired. I did not see where Bulmar was when the men stood on the other side of the 'gruff'. Bulmar was betwixt them and me. I know the country, but cannot say how wide the 'gruff' is.

The prosecutor was quick to ensure that the point was clarified for the jury, and Berry explained:

I did not understand the question when I told Mr Cobbett I did not see them cross over the gruff. I thought he meant did I see them go to the bottom.

Joshua Ridley was a police constable from Oldham. According to his evidence on 11 August, he was on Shalyer [Sholver] Moor and saw Samuel Holt go past the Waggon and Horses public house with some others in the direction of Yorkshire:

I do not know how far it is from Marsden Moor. It was a little after 6 pm. There was a man of the name of Collins and another of the name of Shepley. I do not know that it was the same Collins that was committed from this court on a charge of shooting at a gamekeeper. I know the man, he is in court; I see him now. I made a remark to a brother officer who was with me.

Another policeman, Jonathan Mellor from Rochdale, was also on the moors:

I was on the moor on the 12 August. I saw the prisoner coming down off the moor above the Tup [an inn near the junction]. *It was about 5.30 am. He came into the Tup while I was there with some keepers. After he had been in a few minutes he exposed a bird to the keepers; it was moor game. He said he had got it that morning and asked 'What they wanted with so many policemen?' He stroked the bird down. He said 'some of them would have to pay for it before it was over'. I have known the prisoner since he was a boy. He had a gun with him.*

Mr Cobbett, then spoke on behalf of the prisoner, agreeing that he could not:

... contend that there was not sufficient evidence to warrant the prisoner's committal, yet at the same time, he felt justified in asking that bail might be taken for his appearance, as he was certainly entitled to every possible consideration. Undoubtedly there was the strictest evidence according to the two last witnesses that Holt was in the same

Waggon & Horses Inn, Oldham. The Author

district of country on the same day on which the offence was committed if the offence was committed at all. Holt might be a poacher, but poaching is a trifling offence compared with shooting at a man. One witness spoke to his identity and yet he was running after him at the time and therefore could only see his back, then the morning too was foggy. It was not possible to identify a common man dressed in common clothes under such circumstances. When Bulmar got across the 'gruff' he turned round and the man shoots at him. Now, he could only have seen the man's features while he was in the act of lifting the gun because when the gun was lifted to his shoulder his head would be down, therefore it was only a glimpse that could be obtained and no jury in the world could come to the conclusion that that was sufficient to identify a man. In a case of murder, such testimony could not be taken. Then again, he was only six yards off when the shot was fired, and the bench would recollect the description he gave of the shot rustling about his legs. Now at so short a distance the shot must have entered the ground . . . and must have cut up the ground where it touched and yet when the question was asked as to the appearance of the ground the reply was, he saw nothing in particular.

Holt was then committed to trial on the charge but was admitted to bail, himself for £150 and two sureties of £75 each.

At the winter assizes in December, Samuel Holt appeared in court, as did Joseph Collins who was also charged with shooting. Specifically, Collins was charged with shooting at Miles Schofield, who had also been employed by Dowse to watch the moors as one of the group of gamekeepers.

During the fracas between the poachers and the gamekeepers, it was alleged that Collins had fired the shot which had hit Schofield in the face, though fortunately not doing too much damage.

The defence was that statements made were false since no one knew who had actually fired the shots and in fact the prosecution witnesses had admitted this immediately after the incident had occurred, therefore Collins was not guilty of shooting 'with intent to maim, disfigure or do grievous bodily harm'.

The jury agreed but decided Collins was guilty of common assault. At the later trial of Holt, the jury came to the same conclusion – guilty of common assault.

CHAPTER 13

The Wrong Victim?
1855

His head was bloody and he was moaning 'Oh dear'.

o the north-east of Huddersfield lies an area which once had extensive coal mines – the National Coal Mining Museum for England is to be found here. Sir John Lister Kaye owned much of this land, including the Hope and Blossom Coal pits in Whitley Upper.

William Margison of Shitlington (now Middlestown), labourer and galloway (pony) driver, worked underground between these two pits. On 20 January 1855, he described his last actions of the day:

> *I was driving last Wednesday afternoon about 4 pm, taking a truck of eight corves* [originally woven baskets – later iron wheeled tubs – used for transporting coal] *from Hope Pit to the pass-by near the pit-eye of the Blossom Pit, about 400 or 500 yards. I put on the corves at Hope Pit, pulled out the wooden plugs that keep down the catches to hold the corves on the rolley. There is a rise in the tramway for about thirty yards between Hope Pit and Blossom Pit. The catches are self-acting and I always use wooden plugs or wedges when I fasten down the catches. It helps the rolley and corves all right and I took a rolley full of corves down to the Hope Pit and then I took my horse to the stable. I am the only driver for Hope Pit.*

Blossom Pit had two drivers – George Clegg, a young man of twenty-four and William Backhouse from Shitlington.

Marginson continued:

> *About 6.30 am on Thursday I drove from Hope Pit to Blossom Pitt. About thirty yards from pass-by end I heard a noise as if the corves were falling. The corves are made of sheet iron. I found William Backhouse near the pass-by filling his lamps with oil whilst the noise was going on. I said, 'What's up?' He replied, 'I do not know. I believe the corves are coming off the back.' We both ran forward and found Peter Taylor and*

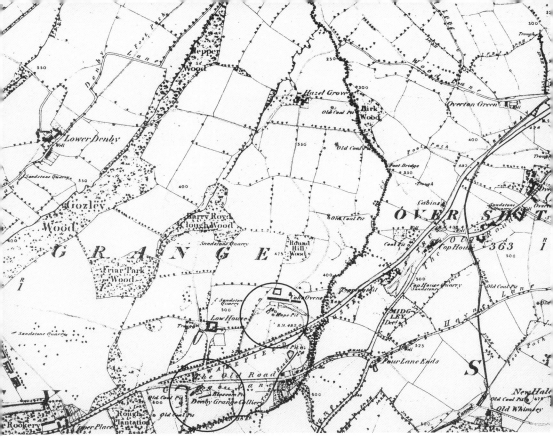

Map (1854) showing the sites of Hope and Blossom pits. Ordnance Survey

Jesse Goodyear holding George Clegg. His head was bloody and he was moaning 'Oh dear'. The truck was off the rails with the front wheels. Seven of the corves were off the truck, lying between the pass-by and pit-eye. The truck was close to where Clegg lay and was fastened against the side by the brake lever. The horse was consequently brought to a stand.

The corves are never coupled on the trucks. The drivers sit in front of the truck immediately behind the horse. I helped carry Clegg to the pit-eye when he said, 'Carry me out of this wind.' William Backhouse went to Clegg's truck and found the catches at the back of the truck wedged down with roof stone so that there was nothing to keep the corves on the truck. When I took the stones out the catches went up as usual. They were the same catches that I had left safe last Wednesday afternoon.

George Clegg later died from his injuries and, at the inquest, held at the Kaye's Arms in Grange Moor, William Backhouse of Whitley Upper, a labourer and driver at Blossom Pit took up the tale:

I saw Margison leave a truck of corves on the Wednesday evening. George Clegg and I took the horses to collect the truck in the morning. It

The Kaye's Arms, Grange Moor. The Author

was my turn to go first but Clegg asked if he could go first as his horse was faster than mine. I began to fill my lamp and Clegg went forward to put the gearing on the horse. Neither of us examined the truck, but as soon as Clegg started off the corves began to roll off backward.

Peter Taylor of Shitlington, a coal miner at Blossom Pit saw the truck go past at speed, with Clegg between the truck and the side.

Seth Metcalfe of Whitley Upper, who was the deputy steward for Hope and Blossom Pits saw Frederick Lister and Richard Mountain working in the pit, as well as Jonathan Webster and Robert Winterbottom, on the night shift. But more than forty men and boys would go down Blossom Pit before the drivers got to the siding from Hope Pit. Any one of them could have tampered with the trucks.

The horse involved in the accident had been in use in the pit for only a month but was used to the procedure. Clegg had worked as a driver for a year and 'was a steady man'. The accident did not seem to be down to error on the part of either man or beast.

When Edward Beacher of Whitley Upper, the steward of Hope and Blossom Pit arrived at around seven in the morning, he found Clegg had been taken into the cabin. He was complaining of pain in his side and leg. Asked how he got hurt, the lad replied:

I cannot tell. As soon as I started the truck the corves began to fall off and immediately the horse increased his speed. I was on the fore end, holding on by one of the empty corves and when this began running back of course I lost my hold and fell off.

Clegg, who was only twenty-four years old, was taken to his home in Grange Lane and died around 9 pm.

Joseph Tatterson, of Lepton, surgeon, was called in and saw Clegg in bed at home. He was in great pain, with a serious wound in his left leg, many blood vessels and nerves being lacerated with considerable haemorrhage. There was also a wound which had separated the scalp from the skull and the fibula of his left leg was broken.

After the post-mortem it was also found that four ribs were broken and one had punctured the lung with internal bleeding. Death was from shock and loss of blood.

Charles Morton, the Government Inspector for Mines for Yorkshire, was present at the inquest, but as the eventual verdict was 'manslaughter against person or persons unknown' no further action was taken against the mine owners.

Hope Pit, Flockton. The Author

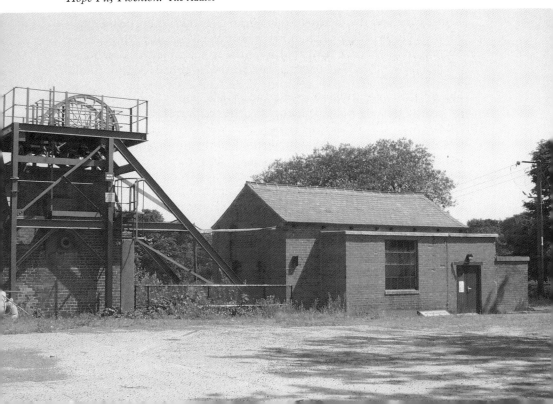

St James' Church, Flockton. The Author

Just who was the 'accident' aimed at? Had Margison deliberately jammed up the safety catch or had someone else sneaked down there during the night and tampered with the truck? William Backhouse should have taken that truck – was he the intended victim? Could William Backhouse have done the deed, and deliberately let Clegg take that particular truck? Was it intended to kill, to maim or merely to give someone a fright, thinking that the driver could have jumped free?

The death remaines a mystery. George Clegg was buried in St James' church, Flockton on 21 January 1855.

CHAPTER 14

Murder or Misfortune? (1) 1852

She appeared to have been badly beaten.

Sarah was born in 1798. The widow of Henry Senior, a labourer, she lived with her four sons and her youngest daughter, Elizabeth, in the village of Skelmanthorpe, about six miles from Huddersfield.

For some time, a young man named Joseph Morley had been 'paying his addresses' to Sarah. Joseph was a weaver by trade and probably well acquainted with Sarah's son, William, who was a bobbin winder. The two young men were about the same age.

About 1 am on Monday 26 April, Joseph went to Sarah's house, rapping on the door until she went down and let him in. At this time William also got out of bed, went downstairs and 'sat in the house with them'. William and Joseph had an argument, though no one knows what about. Finally, Joseph whispered something to Sarah, who went upstairs and got dressed, leaving the house with Joseph. As they were leaving, Joseph turned back, saying to William 'We will let you see who is master when we come back'. That was the last time Sarah was seen alive.

At about 11.30 am, Joseph Fisher, a farmer in Pilling Lane, went to work in his field. At the end of a haystack in the field he found Sarah's body. Hay had been pulled from the stack and spread on the ground, then covered with her shawl. She was lying on her back, and 'Her bonnet was off and her clothes were much disordered'. She appeared to have been badly beaten.

Her body was then taken to the Globe Inn in the centre of Skelmanthorpe, owned by Sarah Gawthorpe, also a widow. Mr Taylor, deputy coroner for the Wakefield district was called to view the body and he immediately ordered a post-mortem.

Mr Field, the court-leet constable and Samuel Scatchard, the parochial constable, went to Morley's house on the Monday afternoon and 'took him into custody'.

Open country around Pilling Lane, Skelmanthorpe. The Author

On Tuesday morning Mr Dowse, a surgeon of Skelmanthorpe and Mr Taylor, a surgeon from Dewsbury, undertook the post-mortem. In attendance was Mr Turton, a surgeon from Denby Dale who had been 'sent to watch the proceedings by the friends of Joseph Morley, who had already been taken into custody'.

The post-mortem revealed marks of 'great violence' on the right side of the head and down the right side of the face, on the neck and right arm, extending down the right side to the hip. On the left, there was discolouration from the neck to the hip, with much bruising on the back as well. The surgeons decided that she had died from congestion of the brain and lungs caused by the violent beating she had received. There was no blood in the heart, which Dr Taylor put forward as further proof that death was caused by violence.

The coroner's inquest heard other evidence. Dr Whitehead said that he had been returning home from Scissett in the early hours of Monday morning, when he had met Morley and they had walked part of the way home together. Morley turned to go a different way and Dr Whitehead asked why, since he did not live in that direction. Morley replied that he 'was going to see Mrs Senior' and 'gave utterance to a most beastly expression'. Dr Whitehead told him to go home, which resulted in Morley making even more indecent remarks.

William Eastwood, who had been in the same room as Morley, after his arrest on Monday stated that Morley had told him that she was 'well and hearty' when he left her.

Joseph Morley then told the court that he and Sarah had left the house together and gone and sat in William Wainwright's cart shed for an hour. They then walked along Pilling Lane into Fisher's field and stayed there another hour. Morley then told Sarah to go home, but she had replied that she was frightened to do so because her son would be angry and said she was going to a relative of hers in Holme, near Holmfirth almost ten miles away. She wanted him to go with her but he refused. He had been 'promised a warp' and must stay to look after it, but promised to meet her in the evening in Cumberworth. He left her at about four o'clock in the morning, by the gate into Fisher's field, when she was 'hearty and as cheerful and laughing as hard as ever he saw her in his life'.

The jury took little time to agree a verdict of 'manslaughter' against Morley, who began to cry. He was committed to York Castle for trial.

The evidence presented at the York Assizes in June was interpreted differently. Morley arrived at Sarah's house earlier than previously thought – about 11.30 pm. The defence, undertaken by Mr Bliss, QC and Mr Overend, pointed out that no evidence of any struggle was found, but there was evidence of sexual intercourse. When Morley was being taken into custody they passed the field and he stated 'That is where I did it, as I had often done before'.

The prosecution insisted that violence had been done. A labourer, James Walter, came forward and stated that he had heard cries coming from the haystack at about 3.30 am and one of the surgeons thought that the bruising was consistent with a beating.

However, the other surgeon considered it to be natural causes. Sarah Senior was fifty-four, had already had at least seven children and was not in good health. It was said that the 'The congestion and overflow of blood into the pericardium might have been occasioned by mental excitement and over-exertion acting on a body not altogether free from disease.'

It was pointed out by Mr Bliss that the defendant could have no motive for attacking the deceased since 'it was clear with what object she left the house to accompany him'.

After a careful summing up by the judge, the jury retired for only a short time before returning with a verdict of not guilty.

Sarah was buried in Cumberworth church.

So what did happen that April night?

If the comments made prior to the trial were accurate, Joseph was at loggerheads with Sarah's children. Could Joseph have tried to make Sarah back him up and lost his temper when she refused? A single blow, rupturing a blood vessel, would have been difficult to detect. If natural causes were to blame it seems unlikely that there would not have been some signs of Sarah feeling ill before the pair split up. Joseph seems to have been a callous young man who saw Sarah as a means of obtaining free sex. If his story is true, he admits that he left her at around 2 am, in the middle of a field. She had said she intended to walk across the moors to relatives in a village ten miles away and was probably complaining of not feeling well. Yet he walked away and left her.

Could one of the sons, particularly the eldest, William have followed the pair and ultimately argued with his mother? Even if no blow was struck, the surgeons agreed that 'great excitement' could have been responsible for the damage. Anger would have had the same effect.

The labourer, James Walter, did not come forward at the original inquest, yet at the trial he said he heard cries in the area at around 3 am. What was he doing in the area at that time? Did he really hear the cries, or was he responsible for them?

Over 150 years later, it is impossible to tell.

Cumberworth Church. The Author

Chapter 15

Murder or Misfortune? (2) 1853

John Whittaker had been seen by a witness to place his foot before the deceased and to give him a push in the back ...

One Wednesday in March 1853, a number of men met at a public house in Lindley. As often happens on these occasions, a quarrel arose between two of them, Blackburn and James Walsh, and they went into a field to fight. Following them were John Whittaker and James Kaye. The fight started but soon Joshua Brook, the constable from Marsh and also Constable Haigh arrived. They proceeded to take the two fighters into custody.

John Whittaker followed and at Dyke End Lane he was seen by a witness to trip up Constable Brook, who fell forwards onto his face on the pavement. When the men tried to raise him up, it was found that he was dead. Whittaker was immediately taken into custody, though he did not try to escape. The others ran off but were later recaptured. Whittaker and also James Kaye, James Walsh and J Blackburn were charged with breach of the peace and bound over in the sum of £10 each plus two sureties of £5 each. Not finding sureties, they were committed to Wakefield House of Correction for one month. Since Whittaker was also charged with manslaughter, John Haigh, solicitor for prosecution, asked for remand until Monday, which was agreed.

An inquest was held at the Plough Inn, where William Greenwood, surgeon, confirmed that he had found no external injury on the body and the brain appeared healthy, as did most of the rest of the body. However, he found the heart covered with fat and 'pale and flabby'. The aorta had ruptured and to this he attributed death, but because of the heart disease a slight shock or fall even without violence would produce death, though Brook might have lived many years with no symptoms. John Whittaker had been seen by a witness to place his foot before the deceased and to give him a push in the back, resulting

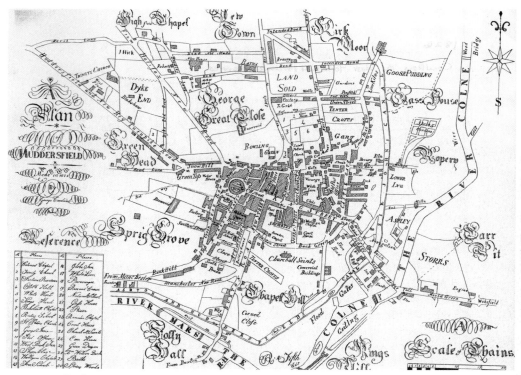

Early map (1826) showing Dyke End Lane, Marsh. Courtesy of West Yorkshire Archive Service

in the fall onto the flagstones. This shock could have brought on the 'heart attack' that killed him.

Whittaker returned to the magistrates' court on the following Monday, where Thomas Brook, the deceased's brother, said he had been with his brother at the Croppers Arms in Marsh on Tuesday 15 March. Joshua was in good health; he'd never had anything but good health.

Joseph Haigh, constable of Marsh, said that on Wednesday 16 March they'd seen some parties fighting in a close near Marsh Bar at about 4.30 pm. Haigh had set off alone but also sent for Brook as he was the other constable of Marsh. Haigh had set off with Walsh to take them to the lock-up, whilst Brook and Blackburn followed. Haigh heard a fall and looked back to see Brook fallen with his head on the causeway and the upper part of his body on the footpath. He'd tried to lift him up and thought he was dead as his face was blue. Whittaker was standing behind Brook. Haigh heard William Bailey

The Cropper's Arms, Marsh. The Author

say, pointing to Whittaker – 'that's the person that's tripped Brook up'. Haigh told Bailey to seize him and saw Whittaker was one of the men he had seen fighting. Haigh said he had known Brook for two years, doing rounds together and he'd always been in good health.

William Bailey of Newtown, cart driver, was the witness who saw Whittaker walking behind the deceased and put his foot out and gave him a bit of a push. Bailey was with his horse and cart opposite the college near where the incident happened. He saw Brook fall, together with the man he was arresting. Whittaker and two other fighters appeared to be drunk. Whittaker was stupidly drunk. A cab happened to be going by so Brook's body was put into it.

Thomas Abbey Bottomley, house surgeon at the hospital, had been present at the post-mortem and corroborated what Greenwood had stated. Death might have occurred at any exertion. Because of the fall plus Brook had hooked his arm through that of another man who was

Holy Trinity Church, Huddersfield. The Author

brought down with him, this would have increased the violence of the fall.

Whittaker admitted he was in such a state of intoxication that he couldn't say what he did or did not do. The jury quickly decided that Whittaker should stand trial for manslaughter and sent the case to York, where the judge and jury differed in their interpretation of the events and decided that since Brook, at age fifty-six, was in indifferent health anyway, Whittaker was not guilty of manslaughter.

Joshua Brook was buried on 23 March at Holy Trinity church, Huddersfield.

CHAPTER 16

Arson at Kirkheaton
1855

He didn't mean to do anything . . .

On 22 September 1855, John Furness was charged with setting fire to a stack of straw in Kirkheaton, the property of Thomas Pickles and others.

Mr Wheelhouse for the prosecution said that Furness had been sleeping in barns and other outhouses during September after a disagreement with his father. He had been seen in the stackyard of Pickles at Fleming House near Huddersfield on two or three occasions, causing worry that he might do a mischief there. He was ordered not to go there again.

Map showing Fleming House Lane. Ordnance Survey

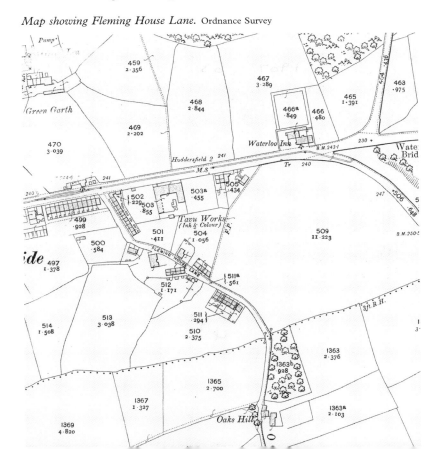

At around 10 pm on 22 September, a neighbour saw flames around the stack and saw Furness running away. There could be no doubt that he did it – he later confessed. The prosecution insisted it was wilful and malicious.

A couple of days later, Furness was apprehended in a wood nearby. At first he said he didn't do anything to the haystack, then said that he'd gone home where his sister had given him 'four Lucifer matches'. He didn't mean to do anything, but when he saw the blaze he ran away because he was 'very much frightened'. He'd run to his father's house, hoping that he could sleep there that night.

In court, he denied saying this – he said that he'd lit a fire nearby and a spark had got onto the stack, but he'd run away because he was frightened.

The jury took little time to bring in a verdict of guilty, the sentence for which was fifteen years transportation. The judge, whilst agreeing that the verdict was right, said that he would recommend that Furness be sent to Reformatory School as he appeared to be a

> ... *poor, neglected lad ... but if he conducted himself properly* [at school] *he would receive a good education and might become a respectable member of society.*

John Furness was just twelve years old.

CHAPTER 17

A Kirkheaton Stabbing 1855

Hill denied knowing anything about the stabbing as he was in a state of intoxication.

In October 1855 Thomas Stead went to the Freemason Arms in Kirkheaton between 7 and 8 pm. At 9.30 pm, a disturbance arose in the house, Alfred Hill being one of those creating it. Benjamin Stead, Thomas' father and the local police constable was called by the landlord, William Raynor (or Reyner). The disturbance was in one of the front rooms and Benjamin went in there. When Thomas arrived, the candles were out and 'pots and candles were flying about'. They were:

> *... poising and hitting my father and I thought they would kill him. I took him into the kitchen and sat down beside him. In a short time the prisoner came in, stripped himself naked except for trousers and shoes and took a run poise at my father. He poised him first time on the hip and second time below the knee. During the second kick we seized hold of the prisoner's leg and threw him down, when he struck me twice with a knife. The first blow went through my coat collar and the second into my side. I fell down and was taken into the room. I was a week at the inn and confined to the home ever since under the care of Mr Marsden of Mirfield.*

Benjamin Stead said he went in to the front room and the noise quietened down so he went and sat in the kitchen. Then they started again and he went and asked them to be quiet. Alfred Hill struck him so he hit back with his staff, then the candles went out and the group attacked him. The rest of his statement corroborated his son's account.

Joseph Raynor, son of the landlord, explained that his father was kicked too during the 'first row and had then sent for Ben Stead'. Raynor senior insisted that Ben Stead go into the front room, which he did, but they wouldn't leave. He confirmed that Hill 'up with his

Freemason Arms, Kirkheaton. The Author

fist and gave Stead a "butt" by the side of his head when Stead turned round and struck him with his staff'. This he described as the 'second row'.

Hill then drew his knife and swore he would stick him (Stead) with it. They got Stead to the kitchen, then Hill and some others came and started the third row, with a run poise at Stead. Raynor gave the alarm that Hill had a knife in his hand, during which time Thomas Stead called out 'he's stabbed me, he's stabbed me'. George Fleetwood took the knife from the prisoner. Raynor went for the surgeon, William Marsden of Mirfield, who found a dangerous wound in the left side and considerable loss of blood. He dressed the wound and attended for several days, refusing to allow Stead to be removed from the Freemason Arms for a week. Fortunately Stead was a healthy character, otherwise the wound might have proved fatal.

Thomas Heaton, another local constable, was called out at 7 am to the Freemason Arms. Stead was in bed, the wound dressed by the doctor. He was given Stead's clothes and the knife, both saturated with blood. Later he went to find Hill at the coal pit where he worked. Hill confirmed that he did stab young Stead, because his father had hit him with his staff. He said his brother-in-law had given him the knife.

By 13 October Superintendent Heaton had charged Alfred Hill with stabbing and he was remanded in custody. On the 27 October the charge was more specific – stabbing Thomas Stead of Houses Hill, on the left side of the back with intent to do him grievous bodily harm, with a weapon 'resembling a Bowie knife or Spanish clasp knife'. Stead was still 'far from recovered'. Hill was sent for trial at York.

At York Assizes in December, Alfred Hill, aged twenty-one, of Kirkheaton, was charged with cutting and wounding Thomas Stead of Kirkheaton on 8 October. Hill denied knowing anything about the stabbing as he was in a state of intoxication, but the court was told about the disturbance amongst the drinkers in the Freemason Arms, Kirkheaton. Hill's defence was that the constable had struck him and that made him excited, but the jury didn't think much of that and found him guilty of unlawful wounding. Hill was given eighteen months in prison.

CHAPTER 18

An Insult Led to Death
1855

Go home, old Shoddy.

On 1 December 1855 James Wharam, worsted dyer, killed his older brother, Jeremiah. Jeremiah was buried in Clayton West, on 4 December. There was never any doubt about the fact, nor did he deny it. The question that the jury had to decide was – was it wilful and deliberate, which made it murder, or was it not premeditated, which made it manslaughter?

News of the murder was reported in the *Huddersfield & Holmfirth Examiner*:

A most foul and unnatural murder was committed between midnight and 1 am last Sunday at the rapidly increasing manufacturing village of Clayton West. The deed has thrown the district into a state of great consternation and excitement, and has excited a painful interest in the neighbourhood where the parties are known. The murder was perpetrated on Jeremiah Wharam, aged thirty-six years, a stuff presser in the employ of Messrs Joseph Norton and Sons and what makes the

All Saints' Church Clayton West. The Author

SHOCKING MURDER BY A BROTHER AT CLAYTON WEST.

Newspaper headlines from the Huddersfield & Holmfirth Examiner. Author's collection

matter still worse the murderer, James Wharam, twenty-nine years of age, a worsted dyer at the same manufactory is the brother of this victim.

The inquest

The inquest was held on Monday forenoon, at the Duke William inn, Clayton West, before Thomas Taylor Esq of Wakefield, coroner for the district and a jury. Mr Thomas Gelder (landlord of the Duke William) was appointed foreman.

Charles Horsfall of Clayton West, labourer, was the first witness examined. He had known Jeremiah all his life. On the Saturday around 10 pm, he was sitting on the langsettle (long wooden bench with a backrest) in Farrington's pub and Jeremiah was standing in the middle of the floor. At about midnight James Wharam came in, just as Horsfall was about to leave. Jeremiah left with Horsfall since they lived next door to one another. Horsfall continued:

When we got to the yard end we came close past James Wharam. He did not say anything as we went past, but when we were about fifteen yards off, James Wharam said, 'Go home, old Shoddy'. Deceased replied, 'That's a word enough to turn back for'. He went back immediately at a sharp walk. It was light. I followed deceased. When I got up he and James had hold of one another. I and others tried to part them and in less than a minute I and Charles Wharam pulled James away. James went away immediately. Deceased said, 'I am stuck in many places. I'm a dead man.' He dropped on the road immediately after James was pulled away. I saw nothing in the hands of either of them. I did not see them strike before they closed. I and William Sheard lifted deceased up and I felt that his clothes were bloody. Deceased never spoke afterwards and died as we were carrying him home, a distance of about a 150 yards.

William Sheard of Clayton West, warehouseman, who was also related to the Wharam family, explained that he worked with James and saw him at his work about 5.30 pm on the Saturday afternoon. About midnight the same night, Sheard was standing at his own gate, just above the Commercial Inn on the opposite side of the road and

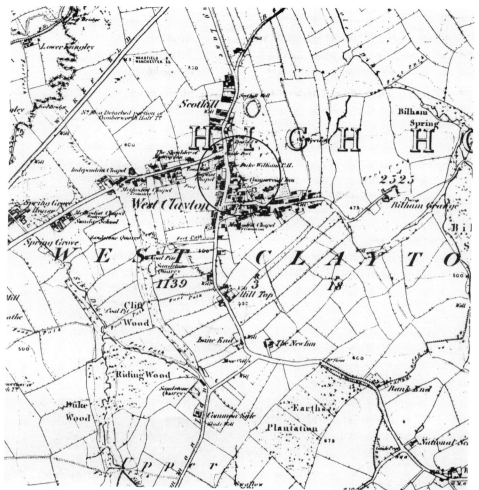

Map (1854) of Clayton West showing site of Duke William and Commercial Inn.
Ordnance Survey

heard the two brothers saying a few words together, though they did not sound to be angry words, until James said 'Go home, Shoddy' or words to that effect:

I heard a struggle and I went to them. Deceased said, as I passed James on the road, that he was stuck all over. My wife brought a lighted candle and deceased spoke no more. I did not start across the road until after the struggle commenced but I immediately opened my gate and walked across the road and found the struggle over. I heard deceased turn back

when James called out 'Shoddy' and I said 'Pray go home, Jere' but he
made no reply. Deceased had got about twenty or thirty yards from
James when he turned back. When I first got up to deceased he was
reared up against another person. I assisted to carry him home and
when we arrived there, he appeared to be quite dead.

Charles Octavious Rowley of High Hoyland, surgeon, was called to
Jeremiah but it was too late. He told the court:

I saw the deceased's body in his own house. He was cold but not stiff. He
was stripped. I observed nine incised and punctured wounds on the left
side of the chest. There were three wounds in front, two below the nipple
and one above and there were five wounds in and under the armpit.
They all appeared to have been made with the same instrument. There
was also a wound on the left shoulder and another at the bottom of the
shoulder blade. They all appeared to have been inflicted with a sharp
instrument. There were two wounds, one on the arm, and the other
below the nipple, about an inch and a half long, and other eight wounds
were about half an inch in length. I saw no other marks of violence
whatsoever. Yesterday afternoon I made a post-mortem examination of
the body. On opening the head I found much fluid blood flowing from
the scalp and dura mater [one of the layers of the meninges of the
brain]. *The membranes of the brain and the brain itself with its*
ventricles were in a healthy condition. And of the wounds below the left
nipple, one passed between the sixth and seventh ribs into the left
ventricle of the heart and the other passed between the eighth and ninth
ribs into the left auricle of the heart. The other eight wounds were not
particularly dangerous. Either of the wounds below the nipple would be
sufficient to cause death in a short time and I am of opinion that
deceased died from those two wounds. A knife, sharp-pointed, would
inflict similar wounds. The heart and other viscera were healthy.

John Bedford, the constable at Clayton West was called and went to
Jeremiah's house where he took 'possession of the deceased's clothes'.
He went on to say, 'I found a knife in his trouser pocket but the blade
was not bloody.'

George Shepley of Scissett, the superintendent constable, confirmed the arrest:

I saw James Wharam at Joshua Riley's beerhouse about 7 pm last
Saturday. He appeared to be quite sober. About 1 am on Sunday I
found John Bedford waiting outside James Wharam's house. His wife
opened the door. James was in bed, apparently asleep. I shook him and
told him I was going to apprehend him for stabbing his brother. He said
'It's a bad job'. I left him in charge of two men and went to deceased's.

On my return James was still in bed. I asked him if he was aware I was going to apprehend him on a very serious charge. I told him to get up and put on his clothes; he did so. When we got downstairs he said 'When I was coming from Farrington's he came up to me and took me a slap between the eyes which made me reel against Bedford's wall. I then went up to him and the job was done'. The prisoner also said 'I can never meet him, but he was always agate of me. He had been at me the last Saturday night before'. I searched the prisoner but could find neither knife nor money. I saw no blood on the prisoner's clothes or on his hands.

William Hardy, a weaver, was next called to give evidence about the long standing quarrel:

I was at Farrington's about three months ago, but I do not know what they were going to fight about. I heard them quarrelling. When James said he would stick him, I said, 'Well, Jem, thou ought to be put in prison for saying it; let alone doing it' He replied 'Go on'.

Hardy continued:

About a month ago as I was passing James Wharam's and I saw James on the causeway about midnight. He said, 'By God, I'll stick him before I go to bed.' I did not see deceased there. I saw William Hall and several other persons there.

William Hall, clogmaker, confirmed Hardy's evidence of the earlier quarrel:

They were quarrelling and standing facing one another. I went away and saw William Hardy on the causeway. I think James had a knife in his hand.

John Burton, a joiner's apprentice, had more damning evidence:

Last Saturday noon I saw James Wharam at Mr Joseph Norton's joiner's shop. He brought a dye-stick to have more made like it. He said he would whet his knife a bit. He asked for the oilstone and I heard him sharpening a knife, but I paid no more attention to him. Mr Norton's men come regularly to sharpen their knives but I never saw James doing so before.

The father, Robert Wharam, a labourer, tried hard to provide mitigating evidence, saying that James had been involved in an accident of some sort about nine years previously. He told the jury:

I went to Mrs Smith's and found my son James there. He was insensible and covered with blood. He was injured on the head. Since that time,

This used to be the Commercial Inn in Clayton West, now a restaurant. The Author

> *when he has had too much to drink he has been very excited. I did not call in a medical man at the time, as James would not have one.*

The inquest returned a verdict of 'wilful murder' against James Wharam, who appeared 'extremely indifferent and insensible to the position in which the indulgence of his evil passions had placed him'. So far did he appear from being affected by the fearful crime he had committed that at the conclusion of the inquiry, before he was removed from the room he said in a careless, bold manner, 'Come, then, let me have something to eat. I'm hungry.'

He was then taken immediately to York where the Christmas Assizes were due to start.

James Wharam appeared before Mr Baron Martin. Mr Hardy and Mr Maude acted for the prosecution with Mr Price and Mr Shepherd for the defence. All the evidence was heard again, the prosecution making much of the longstanding quarrel between the brothers, saying, 'they hardly ever met without angry words'. They stressed the insult James had shouted, 'Go home, old Shoddy.' The insult was obviously enough for Jeremiah, who muttered, 'That's a word to go back for' and went back to his brother. There was a short struggle before Jeremiah cried out, 'I'm stabbed all over.' A minute later he was dead. There were ten stab wounds, with two mortal wounds to the heart.

The jury debated for a long time whether it was murder or manslaughter. If James had insulted Jeremiah with a view to provoking a quarrel and had a knife for that purpose – it was murder, but if it was just a sudden passion, then it was manslaughter. The final decision was 'aggravated manslaughter'.

The judge in his summing up told James his action was 'conduct most cruel and blood thirsty' and as near to murder as possible. He sentenced James to transportation for life.

CHAPTER 19

A Meltham Tragedy
1863

He bought a small hatchet, hiding it under his jacket and 'waited the opportunity to cleave his wife's head unobserved'.

This case from July 1863 was described in the local press as '. . . a case of unusual character [which] transpired in this neighbourhood at the commencement of the week and has excited great sensation, from the fact that it is not often that an event so tragic occurs in this immediate vicinity'.

James Baxter, aged fifty-seven, a slubber by trade, lived at Spark Green, Meltham, with his wife, Mary, to whom he had been married for twenty-six years. Unlike many working men of the day, he was considered a decent, law abiding fellow – generally. But he did indulge in drinking beer to 'an injudicious extent' and then became violent. From this, he was a source of constant trouble and anxiety to his family, which consisted of a couple of grown-up, married children.

For some reason he had became jealous of his wife, despite having no grounds for this, so he decided to take her life. The means he selected for doing this 'were characteristic of primitive barbarity'. He bought a small hatchet, hiding it under his jacket and 'waited the opportunity to cleave his wife's head unobserved'.

One night he came home around 11 pm and found just his wife and daughter at home. His daughter had gone to bed. Baxter wanted his supper so went down to the cellar to get some food, coming up then and telling his wife to get off to bed. Unsuspecting, she turned away, whereupon he took the hatchet from its hiding place and aimed a blow at her head which inflicted a deep flesh wound. The poor woman staggered and screamed that she was murdered and the daughter came rushing into room. Together they struggled, striving to prevent the man from lashing out again. Mrs Baxter received another severe wound in her left arm from the edge of the hatchet, but managed to

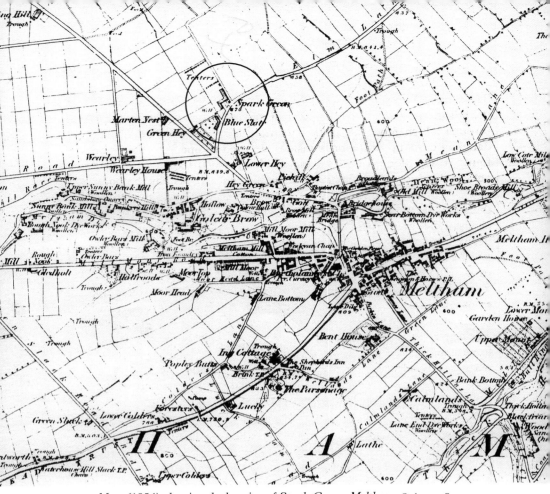

Map (1854) showing the location of Spark Green, Meltham. Ordnance Survey

get hold of him in a headlock, which rendered him powerless, whilst the daughter ran for William Rogers, PC 294, from Meltham. When he arrived he found four or five men outside the house but no one in. Baxter had rushed out and disappeared, so Mrs Baxter had been taken into a neighbour's house to have her wounds washed and dressed. Rogers took particulars – the wounds proved to be fairly superficial – then went in search of Baxter. He found him lying face down in a nearby field and took him into custody. Baxter was totally drunk, but muttered, 'Sorry the hatchet had not opened my wife's skull.' He called her a prostitute and said he fully intended to have done for her; he had bought the hatchet four weeks previously for the purpose. Baxter was taken to the local police station.

A night in the cells had sobered him up so he was in a calm and rational state of mind when he was taken to Huddersfield and put into a cell in the county police station ready for the magistrates the next day. On the Tuesday, PC Marshall went to the cell with breakfast for the prisoner, but was horrified, on opening the little square in the door through which food was passed to the prisoners, to find his body dangling close up to the door inside. He tried to open the door but found it was blocked up with the bedding, which Baxter had piled behind the door to enable him to hang himself, and also by the body itself, which was suspended from a perforated ventilating plate over the door. Marshall ran up stairs for Superintendent Heaton and eventually they managed to squeeze through the door. Baxter had used a black silk handkerchief to hang himself. He'd put a small peg of wood at either side of the perforated pipe to act as a catch to suspend from. No one knew (or admitted to knowing) where he'd got the wood. He had been searched before being put in the cell and had no wood on him then. When he was cut down, the body was still warm, so the surgeon, Mr Clarke, was sent for. Clarke bled Baxter to try to 're-awaken vitality' but had no success. On examining the cell, it was found that the hooks of the ventilator cover which is occasionally used when heat is needed in the court room had been wrenched from their place and also in the cell. Rope had been made from a shirt of the deceased, torn into shreds, from both of which circumstances it was inferred that deceased made an attempt to hang himself from the

Map (1851) showing the location of the police lock-up. Ordnance Survey

ventilator cover hung up by hooks but had been unsuccessful as the hooks gave way under the weight of the body.

Mrs Baxter, who came to court to appear against her husband, did not seem much affected by the suicide but coolly remarked 'they should know where he was now'.

The inquest that same afternoon in the Brooke's Arms, near the railway station, concluded that Baxter had committed 'self destruction' but there was no evidence as to his state of mind at time.

CHAPTER 20

A Point of Law
1864

Could a man firing into a crowd be said to fire with intent to do grievous bodily harm though he had no intention to hit the person injured?

On 18 January 1864 John Fretwell, a wool twiner, returned to Radcliffe's lodging house in Hepworth, where he was staying. At 9.30 pm Radcliffe approached him and announced that Fretwell must leave the next morning. No reason was given and Fretwell promptly grabbed the fender near the fire and hit out viciously at Radcliffe, who was terrified and ran out of the house. A short while later he returned with his friends, but once again Fretwell attacked first, seizing the landlord and throwing him to the ground. The friends rallied round, overcoming Fretwell and finally turned him out of the house. Whilst congratulating themselves on their success, Fretwell suddenly raised a pistol and fired it into the crowd. Hirah (or Ira) Lawton received the full blast of the shot, straight into his face, and for a while it was feared that he would not survive.

Fretwell disappeared, but was eventually caught at Wakefield, where it was found that he still had some shot on him, and this matched the shot that had been extracted from Lawton. Fretwell was charged with 'feloniously shooting at Hirah Lawton at Hepworth, near Holmfirth on 18 January'.

It seemed a cut and dried case. There were many witnesses to prove that Fretwell had indeed fired the shot. However, the prosecution were unable to show that he had actually taken aim when he raised the pistol and fired.

The judge, Mr Justice Byles, was unsure and consulted Justice Blackburn, who agreed that the specific indictment caused some difficulty. The indictment implied that there was intent to do particular harm to a particular person, but it was not proved that this was the case. The indictment also stated 'with intent to murder'.

The questions to the jury were:

1. Did Fretwell aim at Lawton?
2. Did he fire indiscriminately into the crowd without intending to hit anyone in particular?
3. Did he fire intending to hit the people that assaulted him and not Lawton?
4. Did he intend to do grievous bodily harm but to nobody in particular, rather than intend to murder anyone?

The jury finally decided on a verdict of 'unlawful wounding' but the case had to be referred to the Court of Criminal Appeal on a point of law. Could a man firing into a crowd be said to fire with intent to do grievous bodily harm though he had no intention to hit the person injured?

In August of the same year, Fretwell was brought before the court again to hear his sentence. The Court of Criminal Appeal had met to consider 'whether the evidence would support the indictment'. Their opinion was that it would and the conviction was correct.

However, the judge pointed out that 'the prisoner had received provocation and ... the gun was loaded with small shot...', so decided that the sentence need not be as heavy as would normally have been given. Fretwell was sentenced to three years' penal servitude.

It does raise the question of whether the judge was aware of Fretwell's past. Ten years previously, just before Christmas of 1854, John Fretwell and his father, Jonathan, had been in court for a crime which would now probably be considered aggravated burglary.

William Pickford was a grocer at Cross Pipes, Cumberworth near Huddersfield. He lived with his mother, who was eighty-three, sleeping at the front of the house, and a twenty-three-year-old servant girl, who also slept in one of the front rooms.

Pickford locked up and retired to bed around 11 pm. At midnight he was woken by his dog which was ill and need to go out, then he went back to bed. At 2.30 am Pickford heard a noise on the staircase, the bedroom door was suddenly thrown open and three men entered: one with a pistol, one with a carving knife and the third holding a candle.

'Shoot him, shoot him dead,' one cried out, but the other replied, 'Stop, give him time to tell us where the money is.'

Pickford directed them to a drawer in his mother's room. He was held firmly in bed whilst two of the men went off, returning a short while later with the money. They broke open another box they'd found but could discover no more money. Grabbing Pickford by the ears, they dragged him to his mother's room, threatening to kill his mother with the knife until he revealed a secret drawer with a further £35 in.

Next they dragged him downstairs, where they found more money, finally making a haul of £56 10s 6d (£56.53). Pickford was forced back to bed, threatened and told to stay there while they had something to eat. Food and brandy were consumed, and two silver spoons taken when the ruffians finally left.

At 4 am, Pickford finally crept out of his bed and went to tell the constable. Two of the men had gone into the room of Mary

Map (1854) showing Cross Pipes, Cumberworth. Ordnance Survey

Hinchliffe, the servant, and she thought one was John Fretwell but could not swear to it. Pickford, however, was absolutely certain that one attacker was Jonathan Fretwell, a man he had known for twenty years. Fretwell was easy to identify – he had a scar under his lip and a 'contracted' finger.

The constable set off for Fretwell's house in Ingbirchworth, arriving there at 5.30 am. Jonathan was up but John was in bed.

At the Winter Assizes another witness, called Lee, came forward to swear that he had seen John Fretwell, with his younger brother, William, go towards Pickford's house about 9 or 10 pm on the night before the burglary. They returned, then set off again in the same direction. It was suggested that something had been given to the dog to keep it quiet.

The jury decided that Jonathan was undoubtedly guilty, but there was insufficient evidence against John, who was discharged.

CHAPTER 21

Cigarettes and Whisky
1864

William pulled out his clasp knife and lashed out at his father ...

The Sykes family consisted of Joshua and his wife, Ann, who was considerably older than her husband. Joshua had only been seventeen when he had married Ann, then twenty-seven and their first son, William Henry, had been born soon after. A second son, Samuel, arrived four years later, and four years after that a daughter, Sarah. Their youngest daughter, Mary, arrived two years later. Joshua had trained as a woollen spinner, but by 1864 had become a beerhouse keeper in the centre of Huddersfield. He not only had alcohol on the premises, but tobacco for his customers too. And therein lay the problem.

On Sunday 8 May, William Henry, then aged nineteen, wanted some tobacco. He seems to have been a bit of a 'ne'er do well', gaining a job as an errand boy for the railway company, but soon losing that and had become a hawker of pies. He came to the bar of the beerhouse and demanded the tobacco from his sister, who was serving. She refused. Joshua, who was standing further away, heard his daughter cry out, 'Thou dare not' and went over, telling his son to take himself away as he was always causing bother in the house. Perhaps there had been too many 'papers of tobacco' taken and not paid for previously.

William went out of the back door, calling to his mates to follow him. He came back in through the front door, still calling to his mates, but they refused to go with him. Joshua told his son to take himself off, without his mates. William said he would if his father would 'give him his clothes' but even then still wouldn't leave.

The pair argued and Joshua attempted to turn his son out of the house, grabbing him by the shoulder. William pulled out his clasp knife and lashed out at his father, shouting that he would 'have his b***** heart out'. The knife hit the ribs, which deflected the blade, but the surgeon had to be called. He found a V-shaped wound about

The railway station, Huddersfield. The Author

an inch and a quarter deep. Inflammation set in, affecting the liver and requiring 'frequent application of leeches and a reducing diet' but fortunately Joshua survived.

Elias Berry confirmed that he had seen William with a knife when he had been at the railway sheds in Fartown earlier that day. The knife had been lent to William Ackroyd, but Sykes had taken it back. It was an ordinary pocket knife with one blade which appeared to be 'quite sharp'.

Joe Smith Hopkinson saw William Sykes at the top of Quay Street on the Sunday afternoon and heard him quarrelling with his father. Joe distinctly saw William jump at his father and strike him with a knife.

William absconded fast, finally being hunted down in Stalybridge two days later, on Tuesday evening, by Inspector White. His first words were, 'It's a lie. I was cutting some tobacco and he ran against the knife. It's a pity the old b****** did not die.'

Later, his statement to the court was that whilst leaving he'd asked for his clothes and his father had replied, 'thou must go and work for thy clothes, idle devil, same as I do'. He still insisted that he was cutting tobacco and the accident had happened when his father had got hold of him to put him out of the house. The report on the inquest concluded with:

> *The prisoner then went on to make a long rambling statement but was stopped by the Bench who committed him to trial at the Assizes.*

In August, at the Yorkshire Assizes in Leeds, William Henry Sykes, nineteen, hawker of pies, was indicted for 'feloniously wounding Joshua Sykes with intent to do serious bodily harm'.

The jury didn't believe his excuses and found him guilty. He was given four years servitude.

CHAPTER 22

Of Unsound Mind
1864

... kicking out and stamping his foot on the frail skull of the old man.

In the early 1860s Bradley, about two miles to the north of Huddersfield, was still a small village with little more than an inn, a mill and a few cottages. The Colne Bridge Mill had been the scene of a major disaster when seventeen girls died in a fire but was now simply the major employer in the area. Joseph Haigh was a cotton twiner there, working alongside his brothers John, who was a warehouseman, and Thomas, a cotton twister.

Joseph was a tall man, his face unfortunately disfigured by a scar running down the left side of his face, pulling his mouth out of alignment. However, he was a quiet, religiously minded man, who was a good worker and father. Then aged about forty, he provided as well as he could for his wife, Elizabeth, son William and two daughters, Fanny and Alice. The household included his wife's uncle, Joseph Pogson, aged sixty-three, a cotton spinner, who was also known to be a quiet, inoffensive man who had worked hard all his life, putting aside savings which now enabled him to retire. Pogson and his wife, who had died almost twelve years previously, had brought up Elizabeth who was an orphan. The family lived together amicably, sharing the living space. Pogson had a small room at the top of the stairs, whilst the two girls slept opposite. Joseph and Elizabeth slept downstairs in an area known as 'the house'.

However, both the family and the neighbours began to notice a change in Haigh's manner – he became more abrupt, behaving in strange ways and saying strange things. It was feared that he was losing his mind.

On Friday 6 May 1864 the family retired to bed as usual, but in the early hours of Saturday morning Haigh woke his wife, insisting that she help him say his prayers. Together they began to recite the Lord's Prayer, but suddenly Haigh turned on her, accusing her of mocking him and struck her a violent blow in the face. His anger grew, soon

Newspaper headlines from the Huddersfield & Holmfirth Examiner. Author's collection

becoming an ungovernable fury. In fear, Elizabeth ran from the room to where her two daughters were sleeping and tried to bar the door to her husband. His strength proved too much and he forced his way into the room, lashing out at her once again. Fanny, the eldest daughter, screamed out and helped her mother hold Haigh down on the bed to try to contain his violence. Aroused by the screaming and noise, Joseph Pogson came into the room to help, but his presence goaded Haigh even further. He flung off the 'puny hands' of his wife and daughter and attacked the old man, sending him reeling back against a massive wooden chest of drawers. The old man fell senseless to the floor close to the hearthstone. Elizabeth fled from the room to fetch assistance followed by the girls who looked back into the room just in time to see their father vent his fury on his prostrate victim, kicking out and stamping his foot on the frail skull of the old man. Alice screamed again in terror.

Elizabeth ran across the road for help, but when others finally arrived, it was obvious that there was nothing to be done for Pogson. Though he was still breathing, his jaws and the bones of his face were crushed, blood streaming from his ears and nostrils onto the bedroom floor. Though a surgeon was summoned urgently, three hours later Pogson died, never having recovered consciousness.

When PC Thomas Reid arrived and asked what had happened, Joseph replied, 'I have killed the old man.' Later, he was arrested and taken to Huddersfield to await the inquest. He was described as 'still very excited in his appearance'.

The inquest was heard on Monday morning in the Woodman Inn, that being the nearest public building of sufficient size to hold the jury and witnesses. Mr J R Ingram, deputy coroner, presided. Mr Bantoft,

---

Members of the coroner's jury were: James Oakes (foreman), James Scholes, Joseph Hebblethwaite, Joseph Hoyle, Joshua Stoney, William Brown, James Bray, John Hopkinson, John Gibson, William Henry Johnson, William Henry Hirst and James Starkey.

The Woodman Inn, Bradley. The Author

solicitor, was instructed to watch the proceedings on behalf of the prisoner.

Superintendent Heaton brought Haigh to the inquest. Haigh was obviously upset by what had happened, weeping and denying the statements of the principal witnesses.

These, of course, were his family who were naturally very upset. Fanny was the first witness, weeping during most of the proceedings, and appearing 'to be in excessive grief'. She described the evening routine of the household, telling how she had been woken by her mother's screams. Pogson had later come into the room, talking gently to Haigh and trying to get him to be quiet. Haigh then 'took hold of him and knocked him against the drawers . . . he did not strike his head against it more than once'. She confirmed that Pogson had not struck Haigh in any way, but also that she had never known her father strike her mother before either. She was not aware of any quarrels. Haigh took exception to this and asked his daughter, 'Hadn't we had a quarrel the morning but one before this happened?' Fanny replied, 'Yes, you told him to go away and he said he would.' Haigh didn't seem to like this answer either, so refused to ask any further questions.

Thomas Haigh, Joseph's brother, then explained how his sister-in-law had come running to his house at four in the morning, screaming 'Joe is killing my uncle'. Thomas had leapt out of bed, racing across the street in his nightshirt to find out what was going on. Joseph was coming out of the bedchamber as Thomas arrived. 'Oh Joe! Thou shouldn't a done this! What hast thou been doing?' he exclaimed, looking at the blood pouring from Pogson and the bloodstains over his brother's feet and legs.

Thomas got his brother downstairs, leaving him in the company of another neighbour, Joshua Drake, who proceeded to help Joseph wash the blood off his feet, while Thomas went back upstairs to see if he could do anything for the old man. He confirmed that the family had lived amicably until the last few days, when his brother had wanted Pogson to leave the house.

Another brother, John Haigh, was then asked by the judge about Joseph's state of mind. John confirmed that his brother seemed to think everyone 'was in a band' against him, even going so far as to imagine things had been written in the newspaper against him. 'He said they were skitting him and putting stuff in about him. I tried to persuade him it was not so.' John suggested that Joseph had not been in his right mind for a year or more:

I never saw him attempt any violence. That was the reason we let him go at large. I did not think he would harm any one.

PC Reid had further comments to make. On their way to the cells in Huddersfield, Joseph Haigh had said:

I told her two days ago that I should do it. I wasn't master of my own house. I expect I shall be hanged. I have had £50 off the old man. I have always paid the interest of it and I can pay it back. I hope the old man won't die. I did it in a passion.

Haigh seemed quite sensible, talking about his job and the weather.

The surgeon, W J Clarke, confirmed that he had been seeing the prisoner for 'melancholia' some months previously but believed he had got over this. He described the injuries to Pogson's skull as of 'a most fearful nature' and insisting that a sane man could not have caused them. The force needed was such that stamping, with naked feet, on the skull would have caused the perpetrator too much injury.

The inquest jury took only a few minutes to decide that Haigh should stand trial for manslaughter.

On Tuesday 10 May, Haigh appeared before magistrates, George Armitage and J T Fisher, at the courthouse in Princes Street. The same jury attended and the evidence sifted once again. Much was

The old Court House, Princess Street. The Author

made of the prisoner's recent state of mind and the delusions he had been suffering. The magistrates expressed 'regret that greater care had not been taken with regards to the prisoner considering that he had been afflicted with these fits of mental aberration for months past'. The police superintendent was warned to ensure that Wakefield prison were told of Haigh's state of mind.

It was August before Haigh was brought before the York Assizes on a charge of wilful murder, to which he pleaded 'not guilty'.

Little further evidence was brought forth, the prosecution making much of the fact that Pogson had been 'very weakly and diminutive'. He had always paid his board and lodging, treated the prisoner with great kindness and had even made his will in Haigh's favour. However, his brother Thomas now admitted that the 'fits and pains in the head' had been known about since he was only about six years old when Joseph had had his scalp torn open by a combing machine. This had taken over two years to heal. Further stories of mental illness appeared – an uncle had gone to America and eventually drowned himself; a maternal cousin, Abraham Shaw, had committed suicide by cutting his throat four years previously; another cousin, Betty Rawcliffe, had been confined in various asylums until her death. Yet a third cousin, Wright England, was currently confined in Wakefield

Asylum and there was a niece who had committed suicide by hanging herself.

The jury had the final task of reaching some sort of conclusion. There seemed to be no doubt that Haigh had killed Pogson, but was it wilful murder or manslaughter? Had Haigh been aware of what he was doing? Was he sane and therefore responsible for his actions, or insane and therefore unaware of right and wrong at the time of the incident? The question for them was, had it been made out to their satisfaction that the prisoner was of unsound mind at the time he committed the act? That was the important point. What the law termed being of unsound mind was when a person accused, from diseased mind, did not know the nature and the quality of the act which he committed. The surgeon, Mr Clarke, was strongly and decidedly of opinion that the prisoner was not in a state of mind to know the difference between right and wrong, and it was for the jury to decide whether his evidence, coupled with the statement of his relatives, as to the delusions under which he laboured, did not free him from criminal responsibility.

The jury deliberated for only half an hour before agreeing a verdict of 'not guilty on the ground of insanity'.

Haigh was ordered to be detained 'during Her Majesty's Pleasure'.

CHAPTER 23

Murder of a Child at New Mill 1877

There was a wound about half an inch long which had severed the jugular vein.

In 1877, Eli Roebuck, an engine tenter, from Kirkbridge, near New Mill, reported at the County Police Office in Huddersfield that Marsh Roebuck, his son, aged two, had been missing since noon. The father gave a description of the child and how he was dressed. About 12.15 pm a little girl saw the child being led by the hand by a lad whom she described as wearing 'a white slop, torn at the back and fustian trousers, having the appearance of the lad having worked in a quarry'. The information was sent to the Borough Police Office and the lodging houses were searched by the police as it was said a lad answering this description had been seen on the Huddersfield Road, at Honley, and it was suspected that the child might have been stolen for the purpose of begging. The search at the lodging houses did not result in anything.

As soon as it was known at Newmill that the child was missing, a large number of people turned out to search the neighbourhood. The search continued throughout the night and, about 2.30 am on Tuesday morning, the boy was found dead behind the wall bordering Hollingreave Wood, between Newmill and Brockholes, by Henry Cartwright, who was searching for him in company with James Shaw, Joe Holmes, Harry Hinchcliffe, Allen Mellor and Thomas Crosland. There was a wound about half an inch long which had severed the jugular vein. PC Settle was informed and the body was taken home.

Suspicion fell upon a boy named James Henry Stephenson, who normally lived with his grandmother. For the past year he had lived in Thurstoneland with Squire Lee, his father, a quarryman. James continued to use his mother's maiden name since his parents had not been married when he was born. PC Settle arrested the boy shortly after 3 am on Tuesday, taking him first to the local police station and then to the one at Holmfirth. In his initial statement, Stephenson said

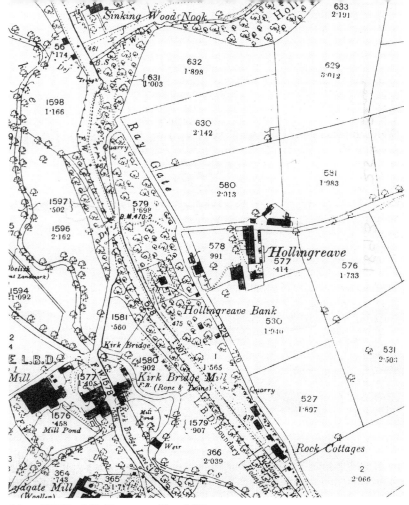

Map (1893) of Hollingreave, New Mill. Ordnance Survey

that another boy had inflicted the wound with a black-handled knife which he threw over the wall into the Newmill Dyke and then kicked him (the prisoner) and ran away. Stephenson was taken by the police during the morning to the spot where the body was found and when he got close to it he pointed to a lane some distance off and said he thought that that was where the deed was done.

The inquest

On Thursday, Mr W Barstow, coroner, held an inquest at the Duke of Leeds, Newmill, near Holmfirth.

Superintendent Sykes of Huddersfield appeared on behalf of the police, whilst R Mellor, a solicitor of Holmfirth appeared on behalf of James Henry Stephenson, aged eleven. The jury started by viewing the body and the place in Hollingreave Wood where the child's body

The jury included: Charles Hirst (foreman), T K Mellor, James Crosland, W Hirst, Edward Ellis, James Mellor, Josiah Thorpe, William England, William Exley, Arthur Bennett, John Heap, George Kaye, Joseph Swan and James Donkersley.

was found. The jury returned to the Duke of Leeds and one of them asked whether they could not insist on the prisoner being present. Superintendent Sykes said it would be unfair to the prisoner and the coroner agreed.

Mary Ann Roebuck, the boy's mother, first explained how the boy had gone missing:

> *I saw him last alive about 12.10 pm on Monday. He was just leaving the house alone. I never saw any more of him alive. I did not see anybody about in the road at the time ... When he went out of the house I was getting the dinner ready. He said he was going out and I told him not to set off ... I began to be uneasy at 12.30 pm and I went out looking for him. I don't think he could have got to the turnpike road in the time he was missing. I went round the mill yard and then I told my husband I would go to Lydgate and to Mr Crosland's on the other side of Newmill. I went on the turnpike road but how soon after half past*

Duke of Leeds Inn, New Mill. The Author

twelve I don't know. I had been looking for the child and met with PC Settle. I don't know at what time I met him.

There was considerable discussion about the distance between the house and where the body was found, in order to establish whether the child could have walked there on his own. The coroner obviously knew the little boy and commented that 'he did not get on well with his walking for his age, he was too fat'. One of the jurymen said the distance from the house to the place where the deceased was found was 200 yards and the place was twenty yards from the turnpike road, suggesting that the child had indeed been helped by someone.

Next, Henry Cartwright of Holme Bottom, Wooldale, woollen pattern weaver, explained how the body was found:

> *I was one of the party who helped to search for the deceased and we found him at 2.30 am as near as I can tell on the morning of Tuesday last. There were seven of us in all searching. I was getting over the wall into Hollingreave Wood. That part of the wood is in the township of Fulstone. I saw the child before I got on top of the wall; the child was laid about a foot from the wall on the inside or wood side. He was laid on his left side and his left arm straight out with his head up the hill and back to the wall. He was same as one asleep. I was picking him up as if he were asleep. I felt that his leg was cold then I felt his face and found it was cold too and I then said 'he's dead'. It was just coming light and we took the lad straight home. We did not notice any blood on the spot. When we got him home I had him on my knee and Thomas Crosland, manufacturer, came and examined him. He noticed that there was a button loose. We saw that there was a hole in the throat and I remarked 'There's been foul play.' His pinafore was very bloody but we did not notice it till we got the lad home. I came up home and Mr Pinck, the surgeon was sent for and immediately attended and examined the lad. I got back and all the search party went back to the place in the wood along with Mr Pinck. We found a stone, and some spots of blood on the wall, close by where he was found. The wall adjoins an old highway leading from Holmfirth to Kirkburton and known as Wray Gate.*
>
> *I was very excited* [in the sense of agitated or upset] *when I found that the lad was dead, because I was overjoyed when I found him and I called out to the others that I had found him. His cap was about six inches from his head.*
>
> *The blood was dry on his pinafore. The wound was small. I thought I could cover it with my finger end. It had the appearance of being cut with a sharp instrument. I don't think it likely that the lad went there himself. It is possible he might get there.*

I can't say whether or not he had the appearance of being thrown over the wall. There is on the wall a mark of blood about twelve inches up the wall. I cannot suppose that the child was thrown over the wall from Wray Gate. We did not find any footmarks in the wood but there were some on the road as many people go that way. There was plenty of grass there. There is a footpath in the wood but there is no right of road through it. The lad was heavy but I can't say the weight. He might weigh three stones. I don't think he could have got there by himself.

In those days there was little consideration of the sensibilities of child witnesses. Sarah Jane Allen explained how she had seen the child being led away:

I am twelve years of age and I live at Lydgate in Wooldale. I knew the deceased personally and used to speak to him. I last saw him alive when he was being 'paddled' by a boy on Monday last. The boy had hold of his hand and was leading him along. It was very near 12.30 pm. It was before the whistles went. I was going with the dinners to Stony Bank [mill] but I was late. The deceased and the boy were just past the bridge at Kirkbridge going in the direction of the turnpike road. I cannot say that they came over the lane. I saw no more of them. He had on a white smock and he had clay-like or dirty trousers as was also his smock. On his head he had a round cap. He was a bigger boy than the deceased. I had never seen the boy before and I did not notice whether he had anything in his hand . . .

Instead of waiting for an identity parade, Sarah was taken straight to Stephenson's home in Thurstonland by PC Settle, she continued:

He took me about 5.30 or 6 am on Tuesday. I saw him after he had got up and I am quite certain he was the boy whom I saw with the deceased. The lad was at the time dressed as he was on the roadway. I did not see the boy's face fully but he turned his face round and I then saw it partly. The child was not crying but was walking on with the lad . . . I did not know Stephenson before. I knew what sort of clothes he had on and a boy named Booth told me that a boy had been to the surgery at Lydgate and he was wearing the same kind of clothes as I have described.

Roebuck and Stephenson were about twenty yards from her at the time she saw them, but she was able to describe the child's clothes as a pink frock, a wincey pinafore and a Scotch cap. She admitted that she 'just casually saw them on the road and I made haste to the mill'. Her identification of Stephenson relied on his smock, which was torn at the back. She stated that she 'didn't see anyone else in the road', though Mr Mellor pointed out that, in fact, there were other children around, going with the dinners to their parents who worked in the mill.

Jonathan Holmes, of Lydgate, woollen manufacturer, who had been injured and was still an invalid, described seeing Roebuck, whom he saw every day, playing by himself in the road, about fifteen yards from his father's house:

> *I was about sixty yards from him. Saw another boy go up to him talk to him a little and then led him towards the bridge. I watched them out of sight over the bridge. Saw Sarah Jane Allen just after they got out of my sight. Boy was dressed in fustian trousers, dirty white smock which was riven at the back.*

He admitted having seen Stephenson on the previous day: 'I had sold the prisoner's father a mule, and it came back and the boy came to fetch it.'

Holmes was obviously a forthright Yorkshire chap. When asked more about his sale of the animal he replied:

> *It was some weeks ago. When I 'geet' the brass for the mule I did not put down the date* [Laughter in the court room]. *I am not sure whether it was a mule or not* [Laughter]. *It was about the time of Holmfirth feast I sold the mule. I am positive about the boy, but I think he had fettled his clothes a bit. I did not see the boy play any marlocks nor cutting the child's throat neither but if I had I would have cut his* [Laughter]. *He had something in his right hand and he led the child by the left hand.*

William Whitehead, Crosland Moor, was a designer working for Lockwood Brothers at Lee Mill, Scholes, Wooldale. He had been sick for a fortnight, then returned to the mill too soon. Feeling fatigued, he told the man who weaves patterns for him that he would go home by train. At 12.40 pm, he set off, walking slowly towards Brockholes Station, then stopped at the bottom of Wray Gate Lane to light a pipe. About eighteen yards away was a child, standing with its back against the wall of Hollingreave Wood and another boy who had in his hand what appeared to be a phial or bottle which he was shaking. Whitehead thought it was Spanish juice water [liquorice flavoured drink]. He took particular notice of the child, which

> *... had nice curly locks and I noticed the face of the child as it seemed so like a child of my own which I had lost. The elder boy was about half a yard in front of him. I thought they were brothers ...*

He described the older boy as having a white smock on, but couldn't see his trousers. The lad had a large face in comparison with the apparent size of his body. When Whitehead went to police station, an identity parade was formed. He saw eight boys, all standing together, and identified the third from the right. Some of the boys had a resemblance to the prisoner, one of them particularly so. He was not told whether his judgement was correct or not, and still didn't know, but Superintendent Sykes confirmed it was prisoner. Whitehead also noticed two delvers going up the wood further on, and later saw a woman, but no tramps.

Hannah Hebblethwaite of Lydgate, wife of Job Hebblethwaite, furnace tenter, next described the events of the morning. She lived under the doctor's rooms, looking after the surgery of Mr Pinck. At around 12.20 pm she had given some medicine to a boy who came to the surgery and asked for 'Harpin's'. The medicine was contained in about a three-ounce bottle and the bottle was wrapped in paper. The boy was dressed in yellow trousers which appeared to be fustian and as if he had been working in stone and a smock which was torn at the back, originally white, but now yellow as if worked in stone. He also had a cap on his head. She had seen him before as he had been for medicine before.

The surgeon's evidence explained how death had occurred. William Pinck saw the child at 3 am on Tuesday. It was quite dead and cold. All clothes were pretty well saturated with blood down the left side and front of the body. Blood flowed from a wound in the neck half an inch above the breastbone – half an inch in length, and half an inch in depth. There was also a wound in the forehead which the mother said had been there about a week. The body was pale and bloodless, perfectly stiff. The wound had missed the windpipe and carotid artery but went right through jugular vein, in a clean cut, done with pointed instrument. All other organs were healthy. The cause of death was haemorrhage caused by the wound in the neck, which could have been caused by a pocket knife blade. It was certainly done with one blow and required some strength to cause it. Pinck confirmed that it was possible the child could have been thrown over the wall – but unlikely.

PC Thomas Settle, from Newmill, confirmed the initial search and finding of the body. He then went to Squire Lee's house at around 3 am. The door was opened by Mrs Lee. When asked if the boy was up, they said, 'No.' The Mother then called out, 'James Henry, get up, there's somebody want thee.' When he came downstairs, Settle went to the other constable who was waiting outside with Sarah Allen and called her in.

'Now my girl, look at that boy but don't say anything.' She looked at him in the face for a short time until I told the boy to turn round.

'Now you can speak if you like.'

She said, 'Yes sir that's the boy that I saw hold of the child's hand at Kirkbridge'. I said 'Have you any doubt?'

'No sir, I am sure that is the boy.'

On being charged with murdering the child, the boy replied:

Please sir, I did not do it, I never did it. That other boy did it, the boy with a fustian jacket on and black trousers. I saw him with a knife in his hand. It was a black hafted knife. The blade was out and the little child had hold of the knife. He put the knife into his pocket. I heard him say he would show him a bird nest and give him what there was in it and I heard him tell the child that he would kill it [the child]. He knocked me down and kicked me. He went down that road between the wood and threw the knife into the dyke.

No weapon was found near where the body was discovered, despite extensive searching of the area and the river, nor was there any sign of tramps on the road, who might have murdered the boy.

The case eventually came to trial at Leeds Town Hall on 4 August 1877. E Tindal Atkinson and F R Armitage prosecuted; Mr Lockwood defended. Mr Lockwood was quick to point out that a crime 'perpetrated by a lad of the tender age of the one they saw in the dock' made considerable difference in the case. As far as its legal aspect was concerned the youth of the prisoner had an important bearing. The law presumed that between the ages of seven and fourteen years a child was incapable of knowing the wrongfulness of the deed he had done. But the presumption was liable to be repudiated by evidence and the questions that would be left to the jury at the close of the case were – whether the deceased was killed by the prisoner; and whether he knew the difference between right and wrong at the time he committed the offence. Before a verdict of guilty could be returned those questions would have to be answered 'yes'.

Further evidence now appeared. On Saturday 2 June Stephenson went to Thurstonland Feast where he bought a knife for which he gave sixpence. It was a brass-hafted, one-bladed knife and bore the word 'Tyne'. Arthur Walton, a boy ten years old, stated that he lived at Thurstonland with his father, and had gone to the Feast with James Henry Stephenson and Samuel Moss, confirming that Stephenson purchased a knife with brass handle, like the one produced in court, but there were a great number of knives on the stall with a similar description. Samuel Moss, nine years of age, also identified the knife.

Samuel Hopkinson, a police officer, stated that he found the brass-hafted knife in a crevice of a wall near the prisoner's house.

This was in the early days of a more scientific approach to solving crimes. There was no fingerprinting, no matching of DNA, no identi-

Thurstonland School. The Author

fication of blood groups. But it was possible to identify bloodstains on clothing and Thomas Scattergood, surgeon and lecturer at Leeds School of Medicine, who was also an experienced analytical chemist, was asked to examine some clothes and 'a left-foot clog' given to him by Superintendent Sykes. He confirmed that the marks on the jacket were bloodstains, irregular in shape and about the dimensions of three quarters of a square inch on the right flap. Small spots of blood were also found under the left arm of the back. The smock also had blood-stains on the gusset of left side. Scattergood could not tell what sort of blood except that the stain was the blood of a mammal. The mark was on the outside of the smock and did not come from the interior. There were also some spots of blood on trousers.

Next, the character of the prisoner was discussed. The head teacher at the Endowed School at Thurstonland, had known the prisoner for five years, for four of which the lad had been at the school. The dialogue went as follows:

'What knowledge have you as to his disposition?'

'It is rather sullen.'

'Are you prepared to state from your own knowledge that he knew the difference between right and wrong?'

Mr Lockwood objected, saying that the schoolmaster may know 'the boy's conduct in school,' but nothing else. The judge agreed that question needed re-wording. Mr Armitage continued:

'Did he receive religious and moral teaching while under you?

'Yes he did.'

'Was his mind of ordinary capacity?'

Lockwood again objected to this.

Armitage tried again. 'Did you notice any particular characteristics?' but Lockwood objected to that also.

The prosecution asked for clarification. 'Can we ask what he found the boy's mental condition?' But the judge didn't like that wording either. 'Ask if there was anything to lead him to suppose he did not understand what he was taught or that his mind was not capable of taking in instruction' he suggested.

The prosecution turned again to the witness. 'You hear that; what have you to say?'

The schoolmaster felt there was nothing to suggest lack of understanding though 'he was below the average. He was not as sharp as some boys are'.

Henry Clarke, surgeon of the West Riding Prison, did not fully agree with this view. He had seen Stephenson since 18 June, spoken with him and noticed nothing exceptional in him with regard to his mental capacity. He could read and write very fairly.

Other evidence was even more controversial. William Tough, a County PC stationed at Huddersfield stated that on 17 June he had charge of the prisoner in the courtyard of the county police station, and Stephenson made a statement to him. The defence took this up:

'Had you spoken to him?'

'Yes.'

'About this affair?'

'No.'

'Why was he removed from Holmfirth?'

'I don't know.'

'Don't you know that the magistrates at Holmfirth ordered his removal to Huddersfield to prevent statements being made by him?'

'No, I don't.'

'Do you mean to say he had never been spoken to about this affair before he made this statement?'

'Yes.'

'Did you caution him in any way?'

'No, I only listened.'

Mr Lockwood remarked that taking into consideration the extreme youth of the prisoner and all the surrounding circumstances, it appeared to him that it would be very unsafe to admit the statement as evidence against the prisoner, but the judge considered that 'this boy has had a good education, and I think, considering his age, I ought to receive it. I also think so after looking at recent decisions bearing on this point'.

For the prosecution, Armitage asked, 'What was the statement then made?' but the judge intervened, asking the constable:

'Did you reduce the statement to writing?'

'Yes, in his presence, in a pocket book.'

'Have you got the pocket book with you?'

'No.'

'Did you take it down as he said it or afterwards?'

'I took it down partly as he said it and partly afterwards.'

At this point, the judge needed to consider whether he should receive the statement as evidence when the pocket book was not produced and retired to consult Mr Justice Lash. Finally, it was agreed that the evidence was not to be received.

Mr Lockwood contended that there was no case to answer. The prosecution had failed to prove 'mischievous discretion' in the prisoner, the capacity to comprehend the nature and consequences of his act, which the law required should be done in the case of a child between seven and fourteen, before a verdict of guilty could be returned. On the contrary, the testimony of the schoolmaster was that the lad was not so sharp as other lads, although this was beside the point. The capacity to acquire knowledge was quite a different matter from his capacity to understand the nature of the crime with which he was charged.

Mr Atkinson argued that the denial of the fact and the concealment of the knife fully supported the presumption of a knowledge of the guilty nature of the act. Mr Lockwood retorted that this was founding one supposition on another, for in order to arrive at the conclusion they were asked to come to, they must assume that the knife was hidden by the prisoner.

The Judge decided that there was a case to go to the jury, at which point the defence asked the jury to consider:

1. Did the boy commit the murder?
2. If yes, whether when he did it, he was conscious of what the result of his act would be.
3. If yes also, at the time of perpetration of deed, was there malice, in which case it would be murder.

Lockwood contended that the evidence was circumstantial. There was nothing direct to show that the wound had been inflicted immediately after Whitehead saw the deceased and the prisoner, as he alleged, at 12.40 pm, and when he arrived home at 1.30 pm. Nothing had been said about the lad being in a flurried condition when he returned or betraying any indications that something unusual had happened while he was away or that there was existing in his mind any knowledge that he had just taken away the life of a fellow creature. Counsel then dwelt upon the absence of motive. There was nothing that could justify anyone in saying there was the slightest reason why this boy should kill his little playmate. There was no quarrel, no tale-telling, so spite, no revenge to gratify. And even supposing they did arrive at the conclusion that the prisoner's hand did the act, he would ask the jury to say that, actuated by some boyish feelings which it is impossible to understand or deduce, the lad having just come into possession of the knife, tried its edge on the throat of the deceased, without any evil intention and, the latter resisting, the knife went deeply in. This was a more rational supposition than the other, that he deliberately robbed the child of its existence. Counsel then proceeded to comment on the absence of evidence of that clear and strong character which the law required before a verdict of guilty could be returned, as to the prisoner's consciousness of the evil nature and consequences of his act. He concluded by appealing to the jury to give the lad the benefit of any reasonable doubts which might arise in their minds, and bring in a verdict of acquittal.

Judge agreed that the jury had a difficult and painful task. They had 'heard an address from the learned counsel for the prisoner, which, he was bound to say, for discretion and power he had seldom heard the like of. It was calm, temperate and with a power of reasoning which brought before them vividly and strongly the material facts of the case ...' and also 'never heard a case more ably and fairly conducted on the part of the prosecution'.

So, was there malice? In order to bring verdict of murder, malice would have to be there.

Was the prisoner the individual who used the knife inflicting the wound that caused death? If so, was he conscious at the time that he was doing an act likely to cause death and was the jury satisfied he really knew right from wrong at the time, so as to be aware he was doing a wicked deed?

After only ten minutes deliberation, the jury brought in a verdict of manslaughter.

The following morning, sentence was given. Mr Lockwood, pleaded that the boy should give a lighter sentence, since enquiries made into home relations of the boy suggested that, 'it was ascertained that the influences he would be subject to at home would be likely to be of a beneficial character'. Also, if he was sent to prison, he would come into contact with the criminal classes and this would most likely make him an habitual criminal. If he were sent to a reformatory his moral and religious training would be an object of special attention and he would be sent out to take his place in the world as a useful member of society.

The judge agreed. The view of the jury:

> ... is that you are a wicked and mischievous boy, who, having bought a knife on the previous Saturday, in a spirit of mischief and knowing that you must do an injury to the child but unconscious that it might cause death, you use that knife and make an incision in the child's throat which caused its death. If you had been older ... you would have ended your life on the scaffold ... the punishment I am about to pass upon you is one which will give you an opportunity of being properly taken care of and properly educated, both morally and religiously, whilst at the same time you will undergo punishment in the shape of hard labour. You will be imprisoned for fourteen days and afterwards confined in reformatory school for five years. Bear in mind that if you get into mischief you will be severely dealt with and if you ever cause death again the sentence will certainly be capital punishment.

Stephenson was sent to the Leeds Reformatory for Boys at Adel, Leeds though whether he did become a 'useful member of society' afterwards is not known.

CHAPTER 24

Terrible Murder in Linthwaite 1891

It was a good face, with a sweet calm expression upon it; and that was the face of a girl who on Friday morning was singing merrily at her work.

When Agnes, wife of George Ramsden, a fettler in Ramsden Mill, Linthwaite, found a job for her niece, it was felt that the girl could do well for herself. Catherine was the daughter of Agnes' brother, Edwin Dennis who was a fireman in a chemical works in Flint and so the teenager was sent from Wales to take up her job in the Ivy Hotel in Linthwaite. Margaret Brook, a widow and landlady of the hotel found Catherine to be 'a good and truthful person; in fact the best girl that ever came into a house – willing, truthful, honest and steady in every respect'. The two got on well together and Margaret had no hesitation in leaving the girl in charge of the hotel for short periods during the day even though Catherine, or Kate as she was generally known, was only fifteen years of age.

On 21 August Mrs Brooke needed to go into Huddersfield. She left around 2 pm, with a carrier, named Charlie Brook. Kate stayed on in the hotel. Two hours later she was dead.

Information was given that two men had been seen in the hotel and within a short time Joshua Lockwood, aged forty-one, and George Farnham thirty, both working for J B Law, a local photographer, were apprehended and charged with the murder. They were remanded in custody, though both denied the charge. Their wives were allowed to visit them and they remained confident that their innocence would soon be proved.

They appeared again in court when it was proved that they had, in fact, been in the hotel during the afternoon, but further enquiries revealed that they had left and later, when the news of the murder had got out, gone back in with the rest of the crowd. They then left and went on to Slaithwaite to the Dartmouth Arms. It was there that Sergeant Ramsden had found them and arrested them. Their solicitor, R Welsh, was most indignant on their behalf, complaining that they were men of good character who had been marched hand-cuffed through the crowd, stripped, searched, kept in prison and all with not a shred of evidence against them. He asked for the case to be dismissed, even suggesting that compensation would not come amiss. The judge was having none of it, merely saying, 'They are discharged and what do you want more than that?'

All murders attract cranks and this one was no exception. Peter Paul Gallagher, a travelling salesman, was 'accused' as a joke by Harry Heywood and George Auty of being the man the police were seeking. He confessed that he was, and began to describe the murder in detail. The men took him seriously and promptly marched him off to Dewsbury Police station, where he was charged and locked up. The next day further enquiries were made and it was found that he had been in the Fleece Inn in Dewsbury at the time in question. Surprisingly, he was simply released, not charged with wasting police time.

Over the weekend, thousands came to visit the area to see the scene of the tragedy. They were conducted, in small batches, through the house to the bedroom where the murder had taken place and from there to the bedroom where Catherine's body was laid out.

The local reporter asked people in Huddersfield, over and over again, if they remembered anyone else being in the hotel, this being constantly denied. But then Mrs Brooke suddenly remembered that there had been another. She informed Sergeant McCawley that a James or John Stockwell who lived in Delph Terrace nearby had been in the hotel kitchen eating bread and cheese and the remainder of a pie which her grandson had had, with a pocket knife. The man was also seen by two others – Mrs Carter and John Walker. Mrs Carter confirmed that when she went out at about 4 pm to find her little boy she saw a 'man with curly red hair and a sleeved fustian waistcoat'. John Walker said he went down to the hotel at around 2.30 pm because Mrs Brooke had asked him to go and pay 'a gas note' for her. Mrs Brooke had already left for Huddersfield, but Walker had gone into the kitchen to see Catherine and the man had been there. Walker left but on his return, around 4 pm, Stockwell had just come out of the hotel.

The inquest was opened, originally in the rooms of the Linthwaite Local Board, but was then moved to the large bedroom at the Ivy Hotel. Mr Barstow JP presided. The body was identified by Thomas

Ivy Hotel – now converted to dwellings. The Author

Williams, Catherine's uncle. He stated that she was generally known as Kate and would have been sixteen on the following Wednesday. It was agreed that burial could then take place that afternoon.

At the inquest, Margaret Brook said that when she left the hotel to go into Huddersfield she had left a man in the kitchen eating some pie. That man was James Stockwell. In the tap room were also Herbert Ainley of Golcar and a Mr Lockwood, who were in charge of horses and carts which were in the stables. They were regular visitors to the hotel, generally eating their dinner there. She commented that Kate was a girl who 'talked to the company'. Mr Dyson asked her, 'Is it likely that he [Stockwell] would pick up that you were going to Huddersfield?'

'Yes,' she said, 'I think he would, because I was going down with the man – the carrier.'

'Did you say what time you would be back?'

'Yes, I said I should be back between four and half-past.'

'Did the girl make friends with anyone outside the house?'

'No sir, she had no followers.'

The jury were: Mr Walker, Mr Dyson, Mr A Hanson, Mr Enoch Taylor (foreman), Mr Joseph Spivey, Mr James Walker, James Sykes, James Quarmby, George Lockwood, Henry Lawley, John Eastwood, Sam Dawson, G H Shires, B Holroyd, A Tinker and J W Crosland.

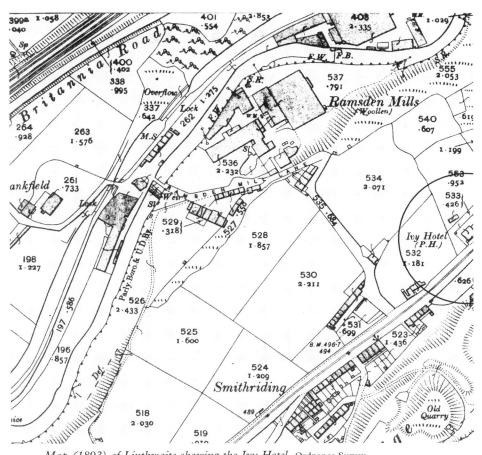

Map (1893) of Linthwaite showing the Ivy Hotel. Ordnance Survey

'No sweetheart?'

'No sir.'

David Beevers, a butcher, was then called. He was employed at the local co-operative store and had called to deliver some meat. He said:

> *I walked straight into the hotel and put the meat on the kitchen table as usual and when nobody came I called out 'Hello!' and got no reply. I looked into the public rooms to see if anyone was there but there was no one and I went to the door. I saw Edwin Hoyle who was just going into the fields and I asked him to look if there was anyone at the back. Hoyle looked and said there was no one about. I went in to the house again and called out at the top of the cellar steps but still I got no response. I then*

went outside and called out to Hoyle that I could not find anyone and I
stayed in the doorway a few minutes. Then I went to Mrs Bailey's and
asked her if she had seen anyone belonging to the house. Someone said
that Mrs Brook had gone to Huddersfield and they hadn't seen the
servant. I told them there was no one in the house and I was told to look
about the premises. I and Hoyle went into the cellar and while we were
there we heard screams upstairs. Mrs Bailey, Mrs Carter and another
woman and Robert Bedford followed me to the house and some of them
went upstairs. After I heard the screams I came out of the cellar and was
told to go to the top landing and I and Bedford went and saw the
deceased laid on the floor. I come with meat every Friday afternoon and
I generally saw Mrs Brook as she paid me. I have never been there
before when they have not heard me as soon as I entered the house. I
know Stockwell by sight but I did not see him at the house on Friday. I
know Herbert Ainley but did not see him there. I did not notice any
strangers about who looked suspicious, because I was on my bicycle and
that took up all my attention.

John William Iredale, a spinner and bandsman in Linthwaite Brass
Band, had been at the hotel between 10.30 and 11 am when he and
Tom Thorpe had gone there to practice. Herbert Hirst arrived later.
They agreed to meet again in the afternoon and went home for
dinner. They met again at around 2.30 pm, drank the beer served
them by Kate and then went on to the Smith Riding Working Men's
Club. Two more men also came into the hotel, but Iredale did not
know who they were. They left before he did. He confirmed that Kate
was all right at 3.15 pm. He also saw a 'stranger' wearing white overalls and a white smock, with a black billycock hat who ordered beer
and went into the taproom. He finally admitted that he had been
mistaken in regard to Farndale and Lockwood, whom he had identified previously as having been in the hotel, but denied ever seeing
Stockwell there on the Friday.

Medical evidence was then given. Thomas Hinchcliffe Haigh,
surgeon of Leymoor, Golcar stated that he arrived at 4.45 pm, finding
the body on the floor of the upstairs landing:

She was laid on her back, with the head in a pool of blood. The head
also inclined to the left and rested on the left arm. The mouth was
partially open, the tongue was between the teeth and face and lips were
pale. On stooping down I found a wound on the right side of the neck
about an inch in length. The wound was slightly oblique and in close
proximity to the larynx. I found no bruises on the head, face or neck.
The body was quite warm when I first saw it.

He then described the result of the post-mortem:

> ... *the wound in the neck ... penetrated the larynx between the hyoid bone and the thyroid cartilage severing the thyroid vessels on both sides of the neck. The wound penetrated one of the vertebrae. There was no blood in the larynx or trachea, showing that the deceased did not die from suffocation. I should say the wound was two and a half or three inches in depth. The cut was clean and I should say it was done by a small and short instrument. In my opinion the wound was certainly not self-inflicted. The cause of death was loss of blood, producing syncope. From the appearance which I saw there had evidently been an attempted outrage, but it had not been successful.*

The surgeon confirmed that a two-edged blade – 'lancet shaped' – had made the wound.

The people in the area immediately organised a subscription fund, since it was obvious that the family were in poor circumstances. Catherine's parents and grandmother arrived from Flint and in the afternoon, the streets of Linthwaite were lined with people waiting for the funeral. A sheet was spread on the ground outside the hotel for

Linthwaite Church. The Author

Kate Dennis' gravestone, Linthwaite. The Author

financial offerings to help the family pay for the funeral. The coffin, inside the hotel, according to the local press, showed Catherine to be

> *. . . a fine girl for her age, with remarkably good features and forehead at the top of which the fair brownish hair showed out of the drapery. The eyes bordered by long, dark lashes and surrounded by finely shaped arched brows, were partly open. The nose was an almost perfect aquiline and the lips parted outwards, showed the two top front teeth. It was a good face, with a sweet calm expression upon it; and that was the face of a girl who on Friday morning was singing merrily at her work, doing*

her duty in life humbly and cheerfully, but who only a short time after-
wards, lay a bleeding corpse, the victim of fiendish lust.

At 3.45 pm the hearse arrived. Press photographers were present too.
Prayers were read inside the hotel and then the coffin, covered in
wreaths, was removed to the hearse and the procession wound its way
to the church at the top of the hill, where Catherine was buried.

Stockwell was declared as being 'wanted' and immediately rumours
began as to where he was. It was believed that he had been in Honley
Wood or around the Meltham area. Stockwell was married, and had
been separated from his wife, but recently they'd got back together.
Mrs Stockwell worked at a local mill, but Stockwell appears to have
been unemployed at the time.

By 28 August no further news of Stockwell was to be had and a bill
was issued by the police:

James Stockwell

A teamer of Milnsbridge, near Huddersfield who is wanted for
having committed the crimes. He is about thirty-two years of age,
5 feet 5 inches or 6 feet high, very fresh complexion, rather stout
build, very coarse ginger hair, inclined to curl, slight side whiskers
and moustache.

Dressed in fustian sleeved waistcoat or vest, fustian trousers,
strong harden apron with a string round neck and black billycock
hat. He may seek employment on new Railway or other public
works. He is fond of boxing and the company of low, loose women.

The inquest resumed on 31 August when W Barstow, coroner, recalled Margaret Brook, landlady of the Ivy Hotel and John Iredale, to
recap their evidence. They then continued with the story.

John Charles Brook, teamer, of Yates Lane, Milnsbridge, the
grandson of Margaret Brook said that he came on Friday about
9.30 am and found Stockwell and Oscar Dransfield in the Ivy. They
all three went for a drink to the Royal Oak and then back to the Ivy.
Stockwell ordered some bread and cheese. Brook had some potato pie
for his lunch and Stockwell asked if he could have some too. Mrs
Brook agreed. Brook left about 1.45 pm, with Mrs Brook and two
children, they all went to Milnsbridge to Alfred Dyson's, then Brook
went home. He said Stockwell used a knife he'd had in his pocket to
eat his pie with. Kate had not been mentioned in any way during the
time they'd been together.

John Lockwood, gentleman, of Springfield Terrace was in the
Royal Oak at 3 pm when a stranger in white overalls, white smock,

black overcoat and billycock came in. They talked about Egypt and he seemed in a cheerful mood.

Other witnesses, Oscar Dransfield, a teamer from Crosland Moor, Herbert Hirst, a weaver, who had gone to the pub to practise with John William Iredale and Sarah Ann Bailey, wife of Thomas Bailey of Smith Riding confirmed the evidence already given. By 1 September, the inquest was complete and after only twenty-five minutes the jury brought in a verdict of murder against James Stockwell and a warrant was issued for his arrest. The police hunted everywhere for him but to no avail.

However, a few days later, on 7 September, Stockwell's mother arrived at the local police station and spoke to local constable, PC Taylor, a young man who had only been in the force three years. She informed Taylor that she had found her son in the house that morning and said to him, 'Oh dear me, lad, hast thou had anything to do with that lass?' Stockwell replied, 'No I haven't, mother.' Though Taylor took a neighbour, Harry Davison, with him as back-up to the little house on Lower Brow Road, Paddock, Stockwell made no resistance, being too exhausted from days on the run. He looked unkempt, still wearing the clothes he had had on the previous week. Taken to the local police station, he was formally charged with the murder by PC Taylor, but Stockwell made no reply. Later he was supposed to have said, 'It is no use going so far round about it. It is all through drink. I was lying down on the seat and she kept pulling my hair.'

The Chief Constable, Mr Ward, and West Riding Superintendent Pickard were also informed of the arrest.

Stockwell was then taken to Huddersfield police station, where he was given food and coffee, later being taken to the yard to be photographed. He was then escorted, along with other prisoners, to the police court. There was a general rush of the public to get into the galleries to view the proceedings. When Stockwell was brought before the bench, he pleaded 'guilty' to the murder. He was then handed over to the county police who transferred him to the County Court where he was remanded in custody for a week.

On 14 September he was brought from Wakefield prison on the 7.18 am train accompanied by PC Webb and PC Battye. A crowd gathered outside the court and tried to rush the gates but the police held them back. Few people were admitted to the court to hear the proceedings but those who were let in included the prisoner's mother, wife, his young son and his sister-in-law. He was allowed to talk to his wife for just a short time.

A H J Fletcher of Laycock, Dyson and Laycock prosecuted and J Lewis Sykes was for the defence. Sykes asked for a further week

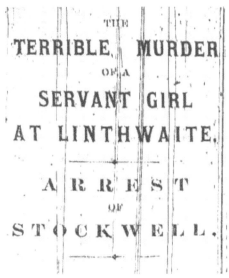

THE

TERRIBLE MURDER

OF A

SERVANT GIRL

AT LINTHWAITE.

A R R E S T

OF

S T O C K W E L L .

Newspaper headlines from the Huddersfield & Holmfirth Examiner. Author's collection

in custody to give him time to prepare a proper defence. This was agreed.

The police van was brought into the yard and the police hustled the prisoner out through a back door to the van. He was then taken to Mirfield station to catch the 12.20 train back to Wakefield. This was done to 'prevent a hostile demonstration at Huddersfield station similar to the dangerous one which took place there when the prisoner was removed last week'. About eighty to a hundred people assembled in Princess Street, hoping to see the prisoner.

The next day his parents made a statement. Mrs Stockwell said that when her son was about five or six months old she had been admitted to Wakefield Asylum for a while. Her eldest daughter, Mary Emma, had been insane for four years and had spent time in Wadsley but was now home 'not right yet but manageable'. Her mother, Harriet Haigh, had died in Wadsley Asylum.

Mark Stockwell, the father, said his brother John, who used to own the Prime Hotel in Huddersfield, had died in Wadsley Asylum. His brother, George, had committed suicide.

A week later Stockwell was taken before the magistrates again and formally charged and committed to Leeds Assizes.

At the trial there was a further surprise. Arthur Thompson, a man of 'medium height, good build and of a sandy complexion' was called by the prosecution. He explained that while at Wakefield gaol awaiting trial he was acting as a voluntary nurse in the hospital where Stockwell was brought on 7 September. Stockwell and he had some conversation as the result of Stockwell asking him what he was in trouble for and when Thompson asked Stockwell what he had been doing wrong he replied 'I have done a murder'. Thompson replied, 'Nonsense, we don't want to speak about that' and nothing further was said until the next day when Stockwell complained of his legs being stiff and said that he had been sleeping in haystacks for sixteen days and had had nothing to eat with the exception of a few apples and beans. Stockwell later began to cry and said he had been thinking of his child and wife. Thompson said he'd told him about the girl he'd murdered – he'd not been keeping company with her, had never seen her before. He admitted that he'd had been drinking and was like a maniac when he was under the influence of drink. He told Thompson that the girl had been tormenting him, knocking his hat off and pulling his moustache and hair and in a moment of passion he ran to get hold of her and she ran upstairs. Thompson asked if anything immoral had taken place and Stockwell said, 'No,' but would say no more after that.

Not surprisingly, the jury convicted Stockwell of murder. J Lewis Sykes, Stockwell's solicitor, sent a plea to the Home Office asking for a reprieve on the ground of hereditary insanity. This was 'not numerously signed but influentially'. However, in January 1892, he received a communication from the Home Secretary stating 'in the usual formal terms that he saw no reason for interfering with the due carrying out of the sentence passed on the prisoner at the Leeds assizes a few weeks ago.' Mr Sykes took steps to inform the father of the culprit.

Major Lane, the Governor of Armley gaol where Stockwell was awaiting execution received a similar note from the Home Office. On being informed of the results of this appeal, Stockwell was said to have 'received the announcement in a dazed sort of way'.

A farewell interview then took place between Stockwell and several relatives including his father and three of his brothers. They arrived at 1 pm and stayed an hour. His wife did not visit but wrote a letter. On arriving at his son's cell, Mark Stockwell said, 'Nah then, James, lad' but he was too 'full up' to continue. Eventually he managed to mutter, 'How are you getting on?' 'As well as can be expected,' was the reply. No allusion to the event was made but Stockwell said he was prepared, and spoke kindly of the chaplain, Reverend Dr Bowlan.

The morning of 5 January 1892 dawned cold and grey with a slight drizzle falling. A small knot of people assembled outside the gates of the gaol together with some pressmen. At about 8 am the black flag was run up on the gaol tower and the spectators knew it was all over, he had been hanged by James Billington. At 8.30 am Under Sheriff Gray said that all had gone according to plan, nothing could be better.

Kate Dennis' mother was so affected by events that she was taken to a lunatic asylum where she died. Stockwell's mother also spent further time in Wadsley Asylum but recovered.

CHAPTER 25

Murder on Marsden Moor
1865

When his son did not come home, he went out again on to the moor looking for him, but Robert was nowhere to be found.

This morning intelligence was received in Huddersfield that a murder had been committed on the moor at Buckstones which lies on the north west of Marsden.

Initially it was stated that William Uttley of Marsden, a gamekeeper in the service of Joseph Crowther of Woodley, Huddersfield, J E Crowther of Royds Mount, Paddock and T H Ramsden of Oakwell, Golcar, who had shooting rights over a section of the Marsden Moor, had been found partly buried on the moors and that Robert Kenyon, son of James Kenyon, keeper who lived at Buckstones had been shot but was alive and had been removed to his father's house, but this later proved false.

The county police office in Huddersfield was informed, whereupon Superintendent Pickard and Mr T H Ramsden started 'in a motorcar' for the scene of the tragedy, even though at that time no one was sure exactly where the incident had taken place. All that could be said was that it was on the moors, somewhere near Marsden and Buckstones.

The local newspaper was quick off the mark:

Through the kindness of Messrs Priest of Lockwood, we were able to avail ourselves of their Daimler motorcar and a representative of the Examiner drove to Buckstones with Mr Walter Priest and they reached there just before 2 pm. They were all wet through owing to having had an encounter with terribly heavy rainstorm going through Outlane and all the way more or less.

The police met John Crowther of Golcar, contractor for a new shooting box which was being built at Buckstones for Messrs Crowther and Ramsden, adjoining the house which was occupied by James Kenyon.

Buckstones house, across the moors above Marsden. The Author

Young Kenyon, who had served as soldier in India, was employed as a teamer for Messrs Platt and Co, Oldham, but was on a visit to Buckstones, staying with his father and to relieve his father had taken part in game watching.

This was the grouse season, when poachers were at their most active, and many men were needed to watch over the moorland. On Wednesday afternoon the two Kenyons went out to range the moor and again in the evening. Apparently they saw a man on the moors and Robert gave chase, soon running out of sight, but the elder Kenyon was not able to follow. He missed his son and went home. When his son did not come home, he went out again on to the moor looking for him, but Robert was nowhere to be found.

The next morning, Kenyon senior asked John Crowther to go to William Uttley's home and see if he could hear anything of him. Uttley was the other gamekeeper employed on the moor so a message was sent to Uttley's house to ask if Kenyon had been there and information was given that Uttley himself went out on the Wednesday afternoon but had not yet returned. Crowther, Kenyon and two young men named William Quarmby (a returned reservist) of

Linthwaite and Fred Garside, set out in quest of the missing Kenyon. The search party left the house at 8 am and went along the moorland road towards Junction and at the boundary turned on to the moor, the four dividing themselves into two parties. Mr Kenyon senior and Mr Crowther, about a quarter of a mile from the roadway in a clough or gruff called Benn Cut, came across a body – not of Kenyon but of William Uttley who was lying on his right side on the heather and it was at once seen that he was dead. An examination of the body revealed a gunshot wound behind the left ear and the cloth of the coat on the upper part was burned as though Uttley had been shot at close quarters.

At that point a messenger was sent by Crowther to Hey Green which is between Blake Lea and Marsden, where there was a telephone, and a message was sent to the police station in Huddersfield.

The search party continued looking and then came across the body of Robert Kenyon, almost wholly covered with earth, stones, sods and heather and only his feet showing. Kenyon senior had with him Crowther's sheepdog, 'Ben' and the animal was the first to give the alarm.

Later, Superintendent Pickard, Crowther and Mr Ramsden went to the gruff. The body of Uttley was taken home to Marsden, and that of young Kenyon to Buckstones.

PCs Smith and Slack with Superintendent Pickard visited the place and Superintendent Prosser from Saddleworth Division arrived with Sergeant Taylor.

Old Mr Kenyon, who was seventy, was 'overcome by the terrible nature of the tragedy' and had to be taken home by some of the search party.

But how did the two men lose their lives? William Uttley, known in typical Colne Valley method of naming as 'Bill o'Mark's (i.e. William, son of Mark),' lived on the moor not far from Blake Lees and Robert Kenyon was staying with his father at Buckstones, a considerable distance away. Both were murdered. Both were employed as gamekeepers. Mrs Uttley and Mrs Kenyon were sisters, thus making William Uttley, Robert's uncle.

The boundary is Moorland Road running from Outlane to Junction above Delph and anyone standing at the door of the White house, occupied by Kenyon at Buckstones could see the wide expanse of moor. In the valley in front is the canal feeding reservoir of the Lancashire and North Western railway company. To the left is the upper part of Blake Lea, beyond is Pole Hill, to the right are the moors at Diggle. The murders were almost within sight of Kenyon's house.

Many men from both Lancashire and Yorkshire frequented these moors. Many had also threatened the keepers – or been threatened by them – and there was often a great deal of animosity between the two groups. Part of the moors were known as the Free Moor or Friarmere where there was no restriction on shooting game, but this ran alongside moorland which was strictly controlled by licence. All too often shooters strayed into the restricted zone, incurring at the very least, the wrath of the gamekeepers and quite possibly, prosecution.

The police visited many places in Lancashire to find these men who frequented the Yorkshire moors. There had been an alleged incident eighteen months previously when keepers were threatened by trespassers on the moors, but all the men had an alibi. A man was arrested at Todmorden, but he also could account for his movements and was released.

It was known that young Kenyon had on him a silver watch but when his body was brought home, the watch had disappeared. If the watch had been lost on the moors in soft peat, it was unlikely to be found.

On Saturday and Sunday crowds of people went to Buckstones, attracted by a morbid curiosity. Large numbers went by trams to Outlane but then the weather turned thundery and so fewer travelled out. Heavy waggonette traffic went from Outlane to Buckstones, and there were also cycles and pedestrians.

On Saturday, the inquest jury went to Uttley's home at Owler's farm and to Buckstones. The inquest itself was held in the offices of Marsden Urban District Council Mechanics' Hall on Monday, starting at 1.45 pm. Small groups assembled outside where there was barely enough room, such was the interest of the press and the area was besieged by reporters. The door had to be guarded by PCs Hirst, Smith and Slack and Sergeant Haynes.

Dr Aspinwall made a post-mortem examination and found Uttley had been shot in the back as well as neck.

A press report described the scene:

At 1.45 pm, James Kenyon, the bent and grief stricken but wiry father of Robert Kenyon, arrived, wearing his keeper's best garments –

The jury consisted of: James Dyson, William Richards, Joseph Beighton, Fred Baker, Walter Metttrick, Tom Boothroyd, Albert Wilkinson, John William Marsden, John Edward Pinder, Thomas Ineson, Sam Bottomley, Dennis Whitehead, John Lees and James Carter.

Mechanics' Institute, Marsden. The Author

*green coat, and vest with shiny gilt buttons and brown mixture breeches
and gaiters, and went inside. Then came Mrs Uttley widow in deep
mourning garments and accompanied by a man dressed ready for
funeral fixed for five o'clock'.*

Later, Mr E H Hill, the coroner, with Superintendent Pickard and
Superintendent Prosser arrived. Over two dozen reporters then made
a rush for the seats. T H Ramsden and J E Crowther were present to
look after the interests of the landowners.

Emily, widow of William Uttley, of Owler's farm said she last saw
William at 2.30 pm on Wednesday when he went out. He'd been out
in the morning but not said he'd seen anyone. He told her he was
going to the top of the moor in the direction of Buckstones. Uttley
worked under Kenyon, watching the same moor, but he did not say he
was going to see Kenyon, nor did he take a gun. His wife had expected
him back about 6 pm. The weather had been fine when he set off.
Uttley was known to be even tempered, had never been threatened by
anyone and was on friendly terms with the other keepers.

James Kenyon then explained that Robert acted as assistant as well as working as a carter for Platt Brothers of Oldham. On the Wednesday morning they'd gone over the moors on the Lancashire side, but did not see anyone then though they did hear five shots on Friarmere. They went home for dinner then returned to the moor at around 3 pm, working towards the Lancashire moor again. This time they saw a man at a place called Benn Cut (or Clough), where the ground begins to go down towards Junction and Benn Clough which lies towards the left coming towards the Standedge side. The man had a gun with him and he was poaching. Kenyon insisted, 'I could tell by the way he was walking,' though he admitted that he was not carrying any glasses. The man was just over the boundary on Friarmere side. Kenyon sent his son after him, though the man was about 600 yards away, telling him to watch an area called 'old gate', which was an old footpath, where the man could get out of sight:

> *I told my son I was going to the gruff and if I wanted him I would give him a signal. I saw the man till he came into gully about twenty yards from our boundary. I gave a signal, firing a barrel. He returned and we went behind the wall. There was a heavy thunderstorm. Then I saw a man about a mile in our land. I did not see any companions. My son said 'Let me go.' I said, 'Wait.' Then he went. I said, 'Now Bob listen if thou gets into close quarters with him you must do your best.' I told him what the man would do to him. I thought I recognised the man and I think so yet. He is a desperate character. I followed my son a short distance. I said, 'Leave thy gun here and go straight on.' I couldn't hear any shots fired, the wind was too strong. I went and took the guns into a workmen's cabin and left them there. Saw Bob go for half a mile and the stranger go out of Bob's path. He was a mile in front of Bob. I did not see Bob again.*

Kenyon then went home, collecting the guns on his way as the workmen were just leaving.

He insisted that he 'saw the man again on Benn cut at twilight – after 10 pm – same man as earlier. I had a dog with me in afternoon but it ran off after Bob and then went home'.

Later, he went out again, putting marks on the cabin wall that his son would know and marks on a stone that he would turn over. At 4.30 am, Kenyon saw Uttley's footmark with a stranger's footmark next to it, which he felt had been made during the afternoon, but he was adamant that it was not Uttley he'd seen in the distance.

He described finding Uttley's body, which was lying face down, his stick still held in his left hand. Uttley had been standing on one of the huts and had fallen straight down on his face. Kenyon could see that the coat was badly burnt about the shoulders, could see his footmarks for some distance, the ground being wet. There were some wads, which were wet, but no cartridges. In his opinion, the wad had been fired within the last twenty-four hours.

Kenyon then wrote down for the coroner the name of the man he thought he saw on the moor – it was his strong opinion, but he couldn't swear at that distance. He'd known the man by his gait and by his footprints, which corresponded to those found. All the footprints were known to the keepers and they'd know when any new ones were among them. The questioning continued ...

'Did you go near Uttley's house in the night?'

'As near as a mile.'

'Why did you not go in?'

'I couldn't have found the way – there is no road from my end near the cabin, also could not have got over stream of water near Uttley's house.'

'Why not in daylight?'

'I was in a hurry to get home to get help to search for my son.'

'Did you know Uttley was on the moors?'

'No.'

Kenyon said he did not think the man on the moor had a hat on but could not be sure.

Ellis Sykes, a cloth finisher from Marsden Clough Lee cottages who had helped find the body of Robert Kenyon agreed that someone mentioned a footprint, but he didn't see any.

John Marsden, also of the search party, saw Kenyon's clogs first, the irons and soles of clogs. The body was lying near a stream, with marks nearby as if something had been dragged. These went back about 400 yards. They also found a place were the stones were moved in order to cover the body.

'Did you see any blood?'

'Yes.'

'Any cartridges?'

'No.'

'Footmarks?'

'Yes, boot marks. It looked as if it had slipped. There were several footmarks, not distinct. The body was covered with two inches of earth.'

'How long would it have taken to do this?'

'Not sure, maybe half an hour. Some stones were taken from six yards away from the body.'

'Were the stones too heavy for one man?'

'No.'

'Did you try to trace the footsteps?'

'Yes, but not far because of the bracken.'

'Didn't you say Kenyon left Uttley's body to go and see the clogs?'

'Yes.'

'Not till after police came?'

'No.'

'How long after that did the father arrive?'

'Not till the police were on the scene. I told him about them.'

'You told the old man but he didn't go for sometime?'

'No, he didn't go till all the lot went.'

'How long after you told him?'

'Ten minutes, perhaps more than an hour.'

'And you didn't know definitely it was his son?'

'No. We took it to be as he was missing.'

'Could the covering have been done at night?'

'No, daytime.'

'Any cartridges, or wads?'

'No.'

PC Henry Thomas Slack who had been on duty and first received the information about the murder, drove to the Great Western Hotel then crossed moors, arriving about 1 pm. There were already a number of people about near Uttley's body, but he looked round and found the wads. Kenyon found one and the police found some. They

The Great Western Inn, Marsden. The Author

also found a key, pocket knife, dog whistle and 5s 11d (29p) in cash. There was no signs of disturbance. It was Kenyon who pointed out a footprint or two but the light made them very bad to see.

PC Oscar Smith informed the jury that he had discussed Uttley's body with Kenyon but nothing had been mentioned about the son, Kenyon only told him about the son when specifically asked. After searching around and finding the gun wads, Smith went across the moors with Pickard and others and James Kenyon. The jury picked up on this immediately.

'Did he lead the way?'

'No, we were all among. I saw a heap of stones, it was said the body was underneath, not disturbed. It looked like a new grave, no earth all stones. Only one layer, I could just see the clogs. It only took a minute or so to throw off. He was laid on his back, head towards Marsden. Found in his pocket a full cartridge, empty cartridge, pair of cartridge pinchers and pencil case and private letters. It would be easy for one man to cover up the body, only ten minutes, I took stones off with one hand.'

John Fullerton Aspinwall, surgeon, first saw the bodies at about 10 pm, and decided that they had been on the moors for twenty-four hours at least. He was not able to say which one had died first. Uttley's face was covered with mud, but there were no grains of powder on his face. He was a strong, muscular man. Though there were no bruises showing, the whole of his upper back was burnt black, owing to the shot. On the left of his neck was a wound an inch below and an inch behind the ear, forming an irregular lacerated wound two inches by one and a half inches in diameter. The direction appeared to be upwards and forwards and there were portions of cotton shirt and wad found in the brain. The wad was about midway through the brain and the base of the skull was shattered with shot scattered over the side of the skull. There was no wound of exit.

Aspinwall gave it as his opinion that the whole charge of shot had gone in and the shot was fired from within 3 feet. He had managed to extract some shot. There were also marks of a shot through the shoulder which had nothing to do with the head wound. The doctor felt that Uttley had probably been knocked down by one shot and finished off by the other. The wound in the shoulder showed a strong shot, a foot in diameter. He was not able to say definitely what the direction was, but it could have been directly behind him and on the same level, around within twelve yards of him. He was also not sure which shot had been fired first, but felt that it was probably not the skull – otherwise why should the murderer have bothered to shoot

Uttley in the back? The shoulder shot had not killed him and he might have spoken or shown signs of life.

At this stage the inquest jury brought in a verdict of wilful murder against person or persons unknown.

In the afternoon, the inquest on Robert Kenyon was held. He was described as 'well nourished, but not strong'. He had a bruise over the forehead, two and a half inches in length. This might have been caused immediately after death in dragging the body, or in falling. On the left side of the neck was a circular lacerated wound about two inches in diameter, about one inch above the collarbone. On the right of the neck, at a slightly higher level, were two wounds, one corresponding to the wound on the other side of the neck but smaller. There was a small opening in front of the larger one, probably caused by a fragment of powder.

'Did you find any burnt skin or powder?

'No.'

'Cause of death?'

'Probably shattered vertebrae.'

The shots were of the same size as those which killed Uttley, and of the same kind, therefore it was probable that one person had killed both. Some shot was handed round for inspection, all of a similar size – five and a half. The wad used was also the same as that found on the ground.

Again, the verdict was wilful murder against person or persons unknown. All that had to be done now, was to arrest the killer or killers.

Just a few days later, they did just that, arresting a man named Henry Buckley on his farm at Graine, near Saddleworth and charged with having been concerned in the murder of William Uttley and Robert Kenyon on the moors near Buckstones. His was the name that James Kenyon gave to the police and also the coroner at the inquest.

When Buckley was conveyed to the central county police station in Huddersfield Superintendent Pickard spoke to him, and he said, 'I was there,' meaning that he was on the moors on the day named.

Buckley was aged forty and married with a family. Strongly built, with a quiet demeanour, he told the Superintendent he was teetotal and a leader of the temperance society in his own area. At one time he used to be an Oldham lamplighter, sometimes doing police duties. Buckley was one of those had been seen by police previously and admitted that he was on the Friarmere moors on the day named, but said he had seen two other men also on Standedge moor. Henry Buckley of Sholver farm, Moorside near Oldham, farmer, was taken before the magistrates at county police court Huddersfield, and charged with wilful murder.

Kenyon also arrived at 4 pm and was interviewed by Superintendent Pickard for twenty minutes, in a small room at the courthouse building downstairs. Kenyon had not seen Buckley at that point but the press there all waited impatiently while a magistrate was found. Messengers had to be sent out on horseback to find them and, just after 5 pm, J A Brooke and J A Willans, two local magistrates, arrived. Pickard then sent for the magistrates' clerk and then Colonel Greenwood, a third magistrate, arrived.

Buckley was brought in and the police asked for remand in custody.

Sergeant Frederick Lee of the West Riding Constabulary said he went to Sholver farm, and asked Buckley to account for his movements on Wednesday 9 September. Buckley said he was at home till dinner time, then left to go to Buckstone moors. This statement was immediately challenged by Buckley, who corrected the statement to 'Friarmere moor,' only to be told by the magistrate's clerk, 'You will have your opportunity afterwards.'

Lee continued, saying that Buckley said he'd arrived on the moor around 2.20 pm. About 3.20 pm he'd seen two men on the moors, but didn't know either. At 3.45 pm he'd shot at a grouse, killed it, but couldn't find it. He'd left at 5 pm and was home by 5.30 pm. On being cautioned, he replied, 'I am innocent. I admit being on the moors but I never saw the gamekeepers.' He was then arrested and brought to Huddersfield.

Colonel Greenwood queried whether he had had a dog, but Lee answered, 'No, he didn't say anything about a dog.'

Buckley again intervened, 'You say you apprehended me – didn't you ask me if I could come forward and try to clear myself?' to which Lee agreed, 'You volunteered yourself.'

Brooke then asked the prisoner, 'Have you any objection to being remanded in custody till next Tuesday?'

'I am at your disposal, if you want to remand me I agree, I am innocent ... I have plenty of witnesses who can confirm that. I never saw the gamekeepers.'

Later, Buckley, looking 'pale and depressed' was conveyed, in the charge of PC Hyde, to Wakefield gaol, taking the 11.53 pm train to Wakefield.

Then something strange happened. On Thursday morning three young men: Rowland Hine, a labourer near Spring Diggle; Robert Edward Hine of Achera Farm and James Albert Riggie of Achera Farm were on the moors when they came across a red handkerchief bundle near the spot where Uttley's body was found. Rowland found it, and when he looked he found it contained a silver lever stopwatch with a metal Albert attached. The watch had stopped at three o'clock and a portion of the glass had broken. The bundle was immediately taken to Superintendent Pickard at Huddersfield. The handkerchief was described as 'Turkey red' – a red border an inch wide, then a white strip about half an inch wide, and two narrow red and white stripes with a red centre spotted white.

As the papers were quick to point out:

The singular part of the matter is that since last Thursday large numbers of persons have been over the very spot where the watch was found.

The police had their own view:

If the handkerchief which has been found on Marsden Moor has belonged to one of the murdered men' declared a member of the W R Constabulary, who had joined in the attempt to unravel the Buckstones Moor mystery 'then we are just where we were.

When the handkerchief was shown to old Mr Kenyon, he 'declared without hesitation that it had been his son's property'. But no one could account for how such a brightly coloured article could possibly have been missed, first by the police and search party and then by the hundreds of sightseers who had trampled all over the moor during the previous nine days. Could this have been planted by the murderer?

In September, the Government appointed J H Turner, solicitors of Huddersfield and Holmfirth to prosecute whilst the prisoner was defended by C E Fripp of Oldham. Mrs Buckley arrived with her son and two daughters, and Buckley was spoken to for some time by General Johnson of the Oldham Temperance Society. Then the prosecution asked for another remand. Fripp asked for bail. He pointed out that Buckley was a man of 'unblemished character' who had served for many years with the police force in Oldham and had been a lamplighter. He had excellent testimonials from both occupations. He was now a farmer. The only evidence put forward by the prosecution was the evidence of Kenyon. The police opposed bail on the grounds that this was a capital charge, and so Buckley remained in custody.

By 25 September, Buckley was in court again, and yet again the police requested a remand, stating that their enquiries were still incomplete. Fripp argued that no evidence worth the name had been brought before the court – the inquiry was taking far too long. The police could have asked for Buckley's clothes when he was taken into custody but in fact they only came for them on Saturday. They were offered the boots, but declined to take them, but on Monday they went back for the same boots. All this was not fair on the prisoner. There were some twenty witnesses present in court – prosecution should present evidence now.

Turner, on behalf of the prosecution, said that the search warrant had not been received until now, though Sikes (the magistrate) denied having received the warrant application previously. Eventually, it was agreed that the clerk would take evidence there and then.

James Kenyon, snr, was brought first. He had been employed for twenty-three years, he said, with Ramsden and the other landowners. Robert was his only child by his second wife – he'd had four children with his first wife but they had all died. Robert was twenty-seven.

There was then some argument as to whether the court should hear information relating to Robert Kenyon only or to William Uttley as well. Finally, it was agreed that all information could be recorded.

Kenyon snr continued, going over the evidence he had presented at the inquest, stating that they saw a man on moors close to Benn Cut, three-quarters of a mile away. 'I recognised him, it was Harry Buckley. I have known Buckley twenty years.' When asked how he had recognised the man he said it was by his walk and the way he carried the gun on his right arm. It was pointed out to the court that most people do this.

This time Kenyon said he gave his son some directions, sending him off to a place called 'Captain Hole' where the ground at that point was higher than the surrounding ground.

Kenyon snr went down the road as far as the workmen's cabin, where there were three or four workmen. He spoke to one whose name was Shaw, and pointed out the man (Buckley) to him.

Here, Fripp intervened and asked for all witnesses to be removed from court. Kenyon confirmed again that he recognised Buckley and said he was nearer than he had been before. Kenyon snr went onto the wall for a better view, but then a thunderstorm came on, so he fired a shot as a signal to Bob, but didn't know whether Bob answered with a shot as the wind was too strong, but then continued by saying that after the signal shot, Bob had come to him. This fact was queried by the Bench but he stuck to the story. Then he said he could see where the man had gone in to the gruff but couldn't see the man. He and his son had taken shelter under a wall, whilst their dog had run off, then they saw the man again, this time on Marsden Moor, not the Free Moor. The man was going towards Dan Clough, heading off over a ridge. Bob stayed a minute or two then set off in pursuit, leaving his gun behind and Kenyon ran down and gave it to the workman, Shaw, then went back on to the moor up Old Gutter Scar towards Benn Cut and Standedge, on his own moor. Fripp objected, saying it would have to be on Friarmere. Kenyon replied that he'd passed over Friarmere to get to near Benn Cut. When he went back, about 5 pm, he collected the gun from workmen. The second time he went out, he stayed out till midnight, as it was full moon that night, just overcast and dark at times. He'd walked across the moors shouting, 'Bob,' calling in at the workmen's cabin around 3.30 am but the stone he'd marked earlier had not been touched. He arrived home again around 7.30 am.

On his way home he saw Crowther, asking him to send a note to Uttley. Kenyon's wife was also there. She had been towards the cabin with the pony and trap hoping to pick him up, but had somehow missed him.

After breakfast, the search party got into the trap, eventually finding Uttley's body at the bottom of the gruff. Kenyon stayed with the body, while a message was sent to the police.

Questioned about how many times he had seen Buckley on the moor – his own or on Friarmere, he said he had seen him on 3 September and threatened to summons him for having taken a bird. Buckley was with James Tetlow and had shot bird on the free moor; Kenyon was with Mr Whitehead. Buckley had shaken his fist. At this point, Fripp said this was not evidence of anything, and Mr Sikes, the magistrate, also wanted things to move on! Kenyon said they'd been 'fratching' all the way down the road and the prisoner had threatened to let his dogs loose on the moors.

Fripp asked again for bail and asked the Bench to put pressure on the prosecution to 'proceed with as much despatch as possible'. Eventually Buckley was remanded in custody and taken by the 5.15 pm train to Wakefield.

By October, there were still arguments over actually starting the case against Buckley. More evidence was taken from some of the witnesses but none seemed conclusive.

Sydney Uttley, William's son, also a gamekeeper, stated that he'd last seen his father at 2.30 when William left.

Frederick Garside, of Lees, Golcar, mason's labourer, saw both James and Robert Kenyon go out. He saw that they both had guns, but did not see any dog with them. He confirmed that it had rained on Wednesday evening.

PC Henry Thomas Slack, who had received the initial message from Garside at 10.15 am on 10 September, described finding the bodies and agreed that it had been very wet on the moors.

Then Rowland Hine gave his evidence. He described going to the moors past Bentley's Farm, under the ridge on Standedge side. He'd stood at the top of the gully and seen red at the bottom, the sun was shining on it, but it was under a clod. When he pulled it out a watch and chain dropped out. It was seventy to eight yards away from where Uttley's body was found and was taken straight to PC Hirst at Marsden. However, he made the point that the handkerchief was not wet though not really clean. It was not in a position to attract notice, but looked 'as if made up and a piece of earth rolled away'.

James Kenyon was then cross-examined, and all other witnesses were asked to leave the court. He denied knowing anything about the handkerchief of his son and insisted that he'd had a red setter dog with him and guns. When asked about his cartridges, he said he used No. 5 cartridges, but didn't know if they were Nobel's – he used empty cartridges and filled his own as required. Asked if his son had fired, he replied, 'No.'

'Did you discharge your son's gun?'

'No.'

'Did anyone see you?'

'Not that I'm aware of.'

Friarmere was frequented by many persons, but if they didn't shoot there was no knowing who was there.

Kenyon described Uttley's daily round, which he knew well – Blake Hey Nook, the boundary with Friarmere. He went each day in the afternoon.

'Would he stop at Benn Cutt?'

'Don't know.'

'But it is a good observation point?'

'Yes.'

'Was the man observed at Benn Cut?'

'No, further away.'

'Did you say previously that the day was very thick?'

'It was bright and fine in the afternoon when I saw the man, Buckley.'

Kenyon admitted that he was nearly 1,400 yards away when he saw him. The defence went on to question him about his meeting with Shaw.

'When you saw Shaw, you had a dog with you?'

'Yes.'

'Did you point out the man on the moor?'

'Yes, I pointed him out. I don't think I said anything.'

'Did you fire the gun?'

'Yes, once – a signal to Bob.'

Kenyon denied saying he'd left the gun in the cabin and insisted that he'd said he took it away with him. He also stated that he'd always recognised Buckley by his stance – his way of walking and the way he carried his gun.

'Did he have a hat on?'

'Can't say. He had a black coat and trousers.'

'Could you see his face?'

'No.'

'Why didn't you tell Shaw you recognised the man?'

'I can work without telling Shaw about it.'

Fripp then asked, 'Why didn't you tell the coroner if you could identify him?' (no reply)

'Why didn't you send for Uttley when you went out again to look for your son?'

'It was too far to Uttley's house.'

Then it was the turn of Abraham Shaw, a workman from Forest Mill, Saddleworth, who confirmed seeing James Kenyon about 3.30 pm, when Kenyon had pointed out the man on the moors, somewhere near where Uttley's body was found. Shaw watched Kenyon go onto moors towards the man and heard two shots on the moor. Then Kenyon came back with his son's gun as well as his own, before setting off again. The workmen sheltered in the cabin and Shaw remembered seeing a man driving a trap, with his daughter and a second man. Shaw, too, had known Buckley all his life, in fact, Shaw's wife was aunt to Buckley's children and he was sure Buckley had not been in the trap. The men finished work at 5 pm when Kenyon came back and asked what had happened to Bob's gun. For some reason, the dog which Kenyon had with him refused to go with Kenyon, who then left the dog in the cabin but it ran off towards Buckstones. There was no stone in the cabin then, but one was there, marked with a letter K, on the next morning, at 8 am.

Shaw denied that the man Kenyon pointed out on the moor was Buckley. The man on the moor was not as tall as Buckley, but it was difficult to tell as he was over a mile away. Kenyon had spoken to him: 'I can never turn me round but I always see somebody on the moors. Sithee yonder' but had not mentioned any name.

When Kenyon had arrived next morning and said his son had not turned up, he said nothing about the man on the moor. One of the other workmen, Joe Wilson, corroborated Shaw's evidence, though he denied there had been any thunder. The other workman, John Ralph Lumb, had examined Bob's gun when it was left in the cabin. It was not loaded but he couldn't say whether it had been fired or just not loaded.

When PC Mellor and Sergeant Taylor had gone to Buckley's house to take the first statement. He had said that his wife and son, Richard, came up with pony and trap about 4 pm, near to Crawshaw Hey Well, and drove him home. About 5 am he'd gone on the moors with Arthur Settle of Delph and two others, for about an hour, but didn't get any birds. They had shot in Jockey Gruff, using mainly eight and six cartridges but also four's and five's. Buckley agreed that he knew 'Stansey' as he called Kenyon and Bill o' Mark's – i.e. Uttley. Kenyon had accused Buckley of shooting on the road and threatened to charge him. Buckley mentioned a number of men who had often threatened to shoot 'Stansey' but didn't think they meant it. Later cartridges were found – all eight's, one of them unmarked.

Ernest Mellor and Greenwood Varley came forward to say that they had both been on the road, sheltering under a wall. They saw a trap with two men and a woman, going up, and coming down, but no trap with woman and little boy.

Then came some damning evidence. John Wheelwright, a farmer at Sholver, saw Buckley return in a trap around 6.30 pm. He was in the bottom of the trap with a top coat over his head. His wife and little boy were with him, but there was only one seat in the trap.

However, on being questioned by Fripp, it turned out that Wheelwright had been accused by Buckley of having maimed some of his cattle and allowing his dog to worry some hens. Buckley had taken Wheelwright to court over the hens and won. Wheelwright did not tell police of seeing Buckley until they went to ask him.

Walter Croad, also a farmer at Sholver, swore to seeing Buckley in the trap, confirmed only one seat so Buckley sat on the floor, wearing his coat over his shoulders. This was around 6.25 pm, whereas when arrested Buckley had said he'd got home about 5.30 pm.

The next day Wheelwright was recalled. He said that on Sunday 20 September he was in the house of Mr Fretwell and discussed Buckley, including his returning home at 6.30 pm. Fretwell's wife had asked how Buckley could be at the Temperance at 6.35 pm if he only got home at 6.30 pm. Mrs Fretwell said Buckley was playing at billiards at the Temperance.

Wheelwright replied, saying, 'I have never been to the Temperance. I don't know what it is.' He said that Mrs Fretwell had asked him what time Buckley got home and had answered, '6.30 pm.' He denied having said, 'I know nothing about it myself.'

Henry Hoyle of Sholver Fold, a beamer, said he was at home on the night of 9 September and he too saw Buckley in his trap at around 6.30 pm. Questioned about the time he said he was sure it was 6.30 pm because of the time he'd had his tea and 'sat a bit' at the window, but admitted he couldn't be sure to half an hour or so. Again, this damning evidence seemed more explicable when it was shown

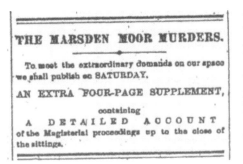

THE MARSDEN MOOR MURDERS.

To meet the extraordinary demands on our space we shall publish on SATURDAY,

AN EXTRA FOUR-PAGE SUPPLEMENT,

containing

A   DETAILED   ACCOUNT of the Magisterial proceedings up to the close of the sittings.

Newspaper headlines from the Huddersfield & Holmfirth Examiner. Author's collection

that Hoyle had been summonsed by Buckley for being drunk the previous year!

Police then produced a red and white handkerchief similar to that found on the moor, which they had found at the prisoner's house. Red and white handkerchiefs were popular at the turn of the century. Many people had similar designs.

William Whitehead then mentioned being with Kenyon and others when they met Buckley at the Old Tap Yard Inn on the high road between Halifax and Oldham. Kenyon and Buckley had 'words' with Kenyon threatening to charge Buckley with shooting on the highway and Buckley threatening to 'sweep the moor' with bulldogs. It was then pointed out by the defence that Buckley hadn't actually got any bulldogs therefore he was just joking. But Whitehead thought they had got over their temper and were friendly when he left.

James Tetlow, who lived at Standedge, said he saw Buckley and Kenyon on 3 September. Kenyon demanded Buckley's licence, and Buckley had said, 'If tha'll give me a shilling, I'll show you the licence.' Kenyon had accused Buckley of shooting on the road, but Tetlow had told him that Buckley had been shooting on the free moor, whereupon Kenyon had accused him of lying. Kenyon had been swearing during this altercation but Buckley had not.

Exact details regarding yardage around the moor as to where different people had been or had been seen were given, but these proved even more confusing. Uttley's body had been found three to seven yards inside the Friarmere border.

Then came the medical evidence from John Fullerton Aspinwall who declared that Uttley had been shot from slightly below, about three feet away. Death occurred between 4 and 6 pm on Wednesday 9 September. He'd been shot in the back first, then in the neck.

Kenyon was then asked if he had spoken to some reporters on the day after the murders, but he replied that he didn't know.

The prosecution case seemed to rest on the fact that Buckley had been on the moors sometime during the day in question and therefore could have committed the murders, despite the fact that they were only able to show evidence of some ill-feeling between Buckley and the elder Kenyon, not his son. The cartridges, wads and shot used for the murder were similar to those found at Buckley's house. Two witnesses had stated that they'd seen Buckley arrive home around 6.30 pm, ample time to commit the murders and get home.

Eventually, the magistrates decided that there was not enough evidence to answer the accusation and Buckley was finally freed, to the great delight of the crowds who already seemed to have decided on his innocence.

The funeral of William Uttley

On Monday afternoon, at St Bartholomew's church, Marsden, William Uttley, aged fifty-six, was buried. Large crowds lined the route and at the graveside. The service was taken by Reverend H W Rodgers, MA. The funeral cortege started at 3.30 pm, with eight people needed to carry it up the steep field from Owler's farm to where the hearse waited. The bearers of the pine and brass coffin were all members of the Royal Forresters' Society, to which Uttley belonged.

The order of procession was: Members of Royal Forresters' Society, hearse, mourning coach with widow and her three children, other relatives, friends and neighbours, including representatives from the employers Crowther and Ramsden, and several gamekeepers

St Bartholomew's Church, Marsden. The Author

from the surrounding districts. The funeral cards carried the phrase 'peace, perfect peace'.

Uttley was buried in the same grave as his mother, father and brother – the two latter also having met violent deaths (see below).

The funeral of Robert Kenyon

There was a huge crowd of spectators in the cemetery at Hurst, his native place, where a family grave was owned by Kenyon in St John's churchyard.

The two previous violent deaths

John Uttley, aged fourteen, son of Mark Uttley of Gilberts, Marsden, was employed as a mule piecer at Messrs Benjamin Sykes & Sons' lower mill at Bank Bottom. In December 1865 his employer, John Carter, spinner, explained that he had been fixing the scroll hand on

The Uttley grave, Marsden. The Author

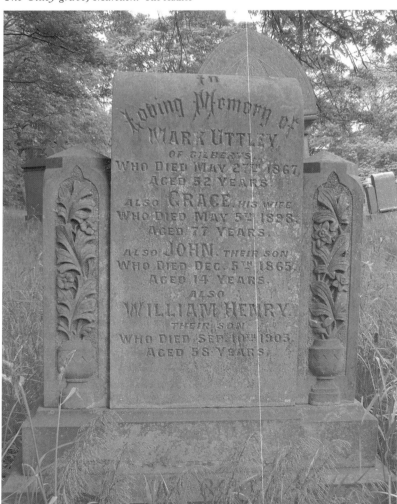

the pulley of his mule so was not actually watching the boy, until his attention was attracted by the boy shouting 'Oh dear' and saw him curling round the horizontal shaft. He ran to get the engine stopped and found the boy on the floor almost dead. Emma Hirst and Jacob Schofield, were also working there and witnessed the events, corroborating Carter's statement.

The shaft is in the attic of the mill and a considerable height from the floor. To reach it the boy mounted on to a platform used for holding empty skeps, with no apparent motive but to amuse himself swinging from the shaft. Unfortunately, the shaft caught in his clothing and dragged him round, wrapping the loose 'slops' (clothes) tighter and tighter round his chest until the cloth broke and he fell to his death below. Part of the apron and 'slops' were later found around the shaft. Apparently the boy had been cautioned against this sort of activity previously but to no avail.

Mr Hesslegrave, the local surgeon, was sent for but pronounced the boy dead. There were no external marks on the body, death being from compression of the chest caused by the clothes being pulled tight. W H Beadon, factory inspector, arrived on Wednesday morning but his report stated that no blame could be laid on the employer.

Barely two years later, in June 1867, his father Mark, met with a fatal accident on Standedge. Mark was a gamekeeper in service of J E Dowse of Hey Green. William Waddington, a butcher, of Sowerby Bridge, was a friend of Uttley and they were out shooting small birds that day in company with Uttley's eldest son. After having some dinner, they stood, leaning against a wall near Redbrook. Waddington had the muzzle of his loaded gun over his shoulder when the elder Uttley went up to him, patted him on the shoulder and suggested that he'd be better going further down the moor. The gun went off, firing the shot straight into Uttley's eye and out the other side of his head, killing him instantly. The body was taken to his home in Gilbert's which was only a short distance away.

The inquest, held on the Tuesday at the Great Western Inn, run by Mrs Rhodes, returned a verdict of 'accidentally shot', stating that there was no blame on Waddington. The deceased was popular in the area, known for his kindly manner and cheerful disposition. He was fifty-two and left a widow and six children.

CHAPTER 26

Drunk and Disorderly Death 1903

Suddenly and apparently without any provocation whatever Carroll, without getting up from the seat, struck the old man a blow on the body and kicked him also in the lower part of the body.

Mid-week at a lodging house in Castlegate was an unlikely time and place for murder. Yet when drink is involved, nowhere is impossible. On 27 August 1903, Thomas Claven, an old soldier, now sixty-five years old, had become a hawker who travelled around the area, staying on a regular basis at various lodging houses, had booked in to Rafferty's lodging house. On the Wednesday evening he went out for a quiet drink, though not, it appeared, a person who regularly got drunk.

John Carroll and his wife had also booked in to the lodging house that night after arriving in the town from Halifax. He was originally a scissor grinder but now had also turned to hawking and had no 'fixed place of abode'. They too went out into Huddersfield for a drink.

All three eventually ended up at the Unicorn Inn in Castlegate. At first it seemed that they had been there 'independently of each other' but it later transpired that they had, in fact, had a drink together. Carroll had bought Claven a drink of beer and possibly a second beer. There was equal confusion over how many drinks Carroll had consumed, the landlord stating just one but Carroll's uncle insisting that he had had 'three or four'.

At about 10 pm, Carroll left the Unicorn Inn and eventually all three went into Rafferty's lodging house. Both the Carroll's were 'under influence of drink' but Mrs Carroll was almost incapable she had had so much. They sat down on a form and Carroll sat nearby. Suddenly and apparently without any provocation whatever Carroll, without getting up from the seat, struck the old man a blow on the body and kicked him also in the lower part of the body. Other blows and kicks followed. Rafferty, the owner was sent for and Claven was helped upstairs to his bed. By morning, he was dead.

On Friday 28 August, at the coroner's inquest, Dr J S Cargin, assistant to Dr Irving, who had made a post-mortem examination said that the cause of death was air in the pleural cavity pressing on the lung, thus putting increased work on the heart so causing failure of the heart's action. There was a verdict of manslaughter but it was decided that the facts appeared to justify a murder charge. John Carroll appeared before the magistrates when the Deputy Chief Constable, Superintendent Hogg said that he had been arrested on Thursday morning and asked for remand of one week which was granted.

A week later at the Huddersfield borough police court, before W D Shaw and J L Walker, John Carroll, twenty-six, was placed in the dock

Map (1851) showing site of the Unicorn Inn. Ordnance Survey

and charged with the wilful murder of Thomas Claven, Mr Wilmshurst of Wilmshurst and Mr Stones appeared for the prosecution.

Ann Claven, of 76 Fairfax Street, Bradford confirmed that the
deceased was her brother. She had last seen him about the middle of
August at Bradford. He was then in good health.

James Watson, hawker, who resided at Rafferty's lodging house was
then called. On 26 August, he said, the prisoner, his wife and the
deceased came into house at 10.30 pm. The prisoner's wife was
drunk, whilst the other two had had some drink but were not drunk.
Carroll and his wife sat down but suddenly Carroll reached over his
wife and struck Claven a blow in the chest. Watson said he did not
observe any provocation. The blow was followed by a kick. Claven fell
over the form and the prisoner then got up and 'closed with him'.
They were clasped together and the prisoner kicked at Claven with
his left foot. Watson heard no conversation. Afterwards, the prisoner
got up and sat back down on the form. Claven struggled to sit up
and said, 'Oh Johnny, what have you done this for?' The prisoner's
reply was a violent kick in his chest. Claven swayed forward and the
prisoner kicked him again, over the right eye. A man called Taylor
then came into adjoining kitchen and when he saw what had
happened he shouted for Rafferty, who came into kitchen. Watson
then went to Claven and advised him to bathe the wound over his
right eye. Claven seemed to be labouring very much in his breathing,
but Watson confirmed that he had seen Claven for a fortnight previous and he had always seemed healthy, breathing correctly. Watson
had then retired to bed and all he knew was that the following
morning he was woken up about 6 pm and saw Claven's body being
carried out on a stretcher.

The chairman of the magistrates asked him 'Were you sober?' To
which Watson indignantly replied, 'I never tasted drink that day.' He
continued, saying that after the affray the prisoner 'picked his wife up'
and said 'we will go to bed'. He then assisted his wife who was in a
helpless condition, through the other kitchen. Mary Ann Watson, his
wife, had been standing by her husband in the bottom kitchen and
was able to corroborate her husband's story.

Next came Margaret Flynn, wife of Peter Flynn who also resided at
Rafferty's lodging house in Castlegate. She had been in the top
kitchen at 10.30 pm and saw the prisoner's wife and the deceased go
into bottom kitchen. When she heard a noise, she went in and saw the
old man, bleeding from a wound over one eye and lying on the floor.
She saw the prisoner kick him twice, violently on the chest, at which
point the witness went out. Claven came into the top kitchen, put his
hand to his chest and said, 'I am killed.' He had to be helped to bed by

Rafferty. Carroll did not look as though he was drunk, but his wife was very drunk. A quarter hour later, the prisoner came to Mrs Flynn's bedroom. She said, 'What do you want here?' He replied, 'I am looking for that tinker. I am going to finish him.' Carroll then examined the four beds in the room to see if anyone was in them. She told him there were only two old women in that room. Rafferty came up, asked him what he was doing and took Carroll to his own room.

John Rafferty, the forty-two-year-old lodging house keeper, had been in his own room at 10.30 pm that night. When told of the commotion, he and John William Taylor, a lodger who assisted him, went down to the bottom kitchen and found Claven sitting on the floor near the end of a form. He was bleeding very fast from a wound over his right eye and breathing very badly. Rafferty had lifted him onto the form. At that time Watson, his wife and Carroll and his wife were in the room as well. When Rafferty lifted Claven up he asked, 'Who has done this?' and Claven pointed at Carroll. Claven seemed in a dazed condition. Rafferty turned to Carroll and asked, 'What did you do that to the old man for?' Carroll just held his head down and would not answer.

Rafferty took the old man to the top kitchen and got him some water and a cloth to bathe his eye with. After that John William Taylor took Claven to bed whilst Rafferty went back to the bottom kitchen and said to Carroll, 'Had you any provocation for kicking an old man like that?' The prisoner did not answer. Rafferty continued, 'I cannot have such work carried on here and if I had known, you should not have come here. Now get to bed as soon as you can and in the morning get away from our house.'

Carroll seemed to have 'had a drop' but not so bad but that he knew what he was doing – he could walk steady. The man then got hold of his wife, who was properly drunk and tried to carry her to bed. The lodging housekeeper got a young woman to help get her to bed. Later he went to see if the man had gone to bed and found him coming out of another bedroom. Rafferty asked him what he was doing there but the prisoner did not make any answer, so he was shown to his room and told, 'This is your room.' Later, the keeper went to the bedroom to see all was right before locking up for the night and found Mrs Carroll partly undressed and her husband pulling her shoes off. Rafferty went to bed at about 11.20 pm. About 5.15 am, John Campbell, a lodger, called him and, on going upstairs found Claven dead in bed. The police were sent for and the door of Carroll's room locked until Inspector Barker came and helped to place the body on a stretcher on which it was removed to the mortuary.

James William Taylor, labourer, resided at Rafferty's, and confirmed the events related so far. He had taken Claven to bed, and given him some warm water. Claven had said to Taylor, 'I don't remember seeing that man before but he has given me my death blow. When you get up in the morning you will find me a dead man.' Though Claven got into bed he could not rest and got up again, saying he had pains in his chest. At about 5.15 am, Campbell woke Taylor up, saying the old man was dead.

John Campbell, slater, slept at Rafferty's. He saw Claven sitting on the bed complaining of pains and was coughing and breathing heavily. He had fetched him some water and saw the old man drink some of it. When he woke up around 5 am, Claven was dead.

Inspector Barker had arrived at about 6 am on Thursday. When he went to the prisoner's bedroom and told him that he was required to go to the police station, the prisoner had asked, 'What for?' Barker said, 'There is an old man lying dead in the room and it is alleged that you caused his death.' 'I know nothing about the old man, I never touched him,' was the reply. At the police station, Carroll was charged with causing the death of Thomas Claven. Carroll replied, 'I am not guilty, sir. We were drinking together in a public house.'

The Chairman of the magistrates made the comment that it was strange that the old man was so seriously injured but no one had been brought to attend him. At this point the prisoner asked, 'Could his ribs have been broken by falling on the form?' But the surgeon did not think this was possible.

John William Brown, landlord of Unicorn Inn, stated that on the night in question, the prisoner, his wife and the deceased were drinking together at his house. They did not visit the house together, nor leave together. The deceased left house first, about 9 pm, then the prisoner's wife left, then the prisoner followed. The latter was not drunk. The prisoner had one pint of beer, paid for his uncle a pint and also paid for the deceased to have another pint. The publican did not hear any angry words.

Thomas Carroll, a tin-plate worker and the prisoner's uncle, stated that Carroll had three or four pints of beer whilst in his company. Thomas had spent some money in drink that he had been keeping to get some stuff to go out hawking with. The prisoner was drunk when he left him but the deceased was too.

Margaret Carroll, the prisoner's wife, said her husband had been very drunk. She did not remember any more.

Carroll was finally committed for trial at the assizes on a charge of murder.

Town Hall, Leeds. The Author

At Leeds Town Hall, on 10 December 1903 before Mr Justice Darling, Carroll was tried for murder.

All the facts of case were repeated and it was agreed that all participants were drunk at the time. The court was amazed that the prisoner had paid for a drink for the deceased at the Unicorn Inn and they had seemed to be on good terms beforehand. There appeared to be no motive.

Mr Mellor and Mr Waddy, for the prosecution, had agreed beforehand that a verdict of manslaughter would be acceptable 'in the interests of justice' and the prisoner's representative, Bruce Williamson, for the defence, said that the prisoner would plead guilty to a charge of manslaughter.

The judge agreed that the court could take into account the fact that Carroll had not met Claven before, and had no recollection of the events. Though drink could not be any excuse, yet it must be taken into account. The prisoner had no intention of causing so much harm and the deceased should have been properly attended to, when he would probably have recovered. It was clear that the prisoner, witnesses and the deceased were all in a state that 'rendered them all more or less incapable of exercising ordinary control but drunkenness was no excuse for crime though it had a bearing on what a person's intentions were'. The judge considered that the prisoner was guilty of 'unjustified and unprovoked violence' towards the deceased and therefore he must pass a severe sentence on him in order to let other persons know that they could not kill others and then say 'Oh I beg your pardon, I was drunk at the time I did it'. Carroll was sentenced to seven years penal servitude.

CHAPTER 27

A Housekeeper Harmed 1903

Rose, I shall take your life if you don't give up working for him ...

On 10 November 1903, Rose Ann Smith, aged thirty-nine, appeared in court in Huddersfield, charged by Jonathan Battye Eastwood, a fifty-one-year-old chimney sweep, of Norridge Bottom, Holmfirth, with wilful damage to a window. She pleaded guilty.

According to Eastwood, on 30 September Smith had thrown stones through his window, then broken the frame with an iron umbrella stand. The amount of damage came to 17s 6d (88p), which Smith had already paid. Smith had gone to work for Eastwood as a housekeeper but he had 'used her and her child shamefully. He held her down by the roots of her hair for three-quarters of an hour ...', before people had interfered and cried shame on him. When the Bench commented that it was very wrong of him to behave in this way, Eastwood indignantly replied that 'that is not the case we are trying now'.

Smith stated again that she had had great provocation and 'if he had only given me and my child our clothes, I should have gone away at once'.

The Bench fined her £1 6s 6d (£1.33), plus costs, which seems a large amount considering the treatment she had suffered. Her new employer, John Battye, also of Norridge Bottom, confirmed that the amount would be paid immediately.

However, this was not the end of the matter. On Monday 16 November 1903, at about 11 am, Smith stood upon a wall at Battye's lodging house, cleaning the clothes line. Eastwood came to her and said, 'Rose, I shall take your life if you don't give up working for him. I shall stop you working for anyone else,' then turned to her child and commented 'You won't cry much longer' and threatened it with a revolver. The woman jumped from the wall to defend her child and Eastwood then discharged the revolver point blank at her face. She

Norridge Bottom, Holmfirth. The Author

felt 'something like burning ashes strike' her face causing wounds in the centre of the forehead and under the right eye. Smith immediately rushed with the child to the door, where she fainted, whilst Eastwood bolted but the police – Sergeant Hudson and PC Barker – chased after him, catching the man near the Victoria Inn and then took him into custody. Mr C R Hampshire who heard the report of the revolver gave first aid to the woman until the arrival of Dr Edward Trotter, who ordered her to be taken to the Huddersfield infirmary in the Victoria horse ambulance carriage.

The case was sent to Leeds Town Hall crown court where it was heard on 8 December 1903 by Mr Justice Darling. Mr Simpson prosecuted.

John Batty corroborated the evidence. He followed the prisoner who threatened to kill him. They had a struggle. Sergeant Batty arrested Eastwood who admitted the shooting and said he was sorry he had not killed Smith.

On being questioned, Eastwood said that he had had no intention of shooting. He had merely been putting his hand into his pocket to get a penny for the child and in pulling out his handkerchief the pistol exploded.

The jury found him guilty of wounding with intent to do grievous bodily harm.

In passing sentence of twelve months with hard labour, his lordship said Eastwood had been convicted twenty-six times for drunkenness and assaults, was evidently a violent man, and had he used the revolver instead of the small pistol sentence would have been heavier.

CHAPTER 28

Death in the Cells 1914

He confirmed that it would not need a great deal of violence, but was not caused by a blow from a fist.

About 2.45 pm on Saturday 17 October 1914, Hettie McArthur was quietly walking down Kirkgate near to Denton Lane, not far from where she lived in Rosemary Lane in the centre of Huddersfield, and not far from the new tenements recently completed. Two men were also in the area. All of a sudden one of them struck the other a blow under the chin. This appeared to have no effect but on being asked 'What have you done that for?' a second blow was struck and the man collapsed on the pavement, striking his head on the stone. Hettie ran towards them, causing the attacker to run away. Carefully, she tended to the stricken man, and sent onlookers for some brandy. He appeared to have sustained only a bruise, but was dazed and unable to stand. Three policemen appeared, and she told them what had happened. Evelyn Helliwell, also of Rosemary Lane and Charles Wells, a baker from Wakefield Road, saw what had happened and confirmed Hettie's statement, though Wells said both men appeared to be 'fresh'. The police too tried to raise the man, who was unable to stand up. Finally they called for a hand cart and took him to the police station. Once there they simply locked him up and charged him with drunkenness. His name was Ingham Spencer, a woollen fettler. He appeared to recover from the effects of drink but when the police visited him in the cell early next morning they found him lying on the floor, unconscious. The police surgeon was sent for and Spencer was taken to the hospital at Crosland Moor, where he died later that day.

The inquest was held on 20 October when Spencer's body was identified by his brother, Robert John Spencer, a scribbling engineer. He told the court that Ingham was fifty-five years old and lived in High Street, Huddersfield but that he had not seen him for four or five months.

Map (1893) showing site of Rosemary Lane/Denton Lane. Ordnance Survey

Dr H G Tansley of Crosland Moor Workhouse Hospital (now St Luke's Hospital) confirmed Spencer had been admitted to the hospital at 9.40 am on Sunday 18 October, unconscious. There was a bruise the size of a five shilling piece on the back, left of his head. He had died at 4 pm. There was no smell of alcohol, but any taken the previous day would not be observable. The post-mortem showed that he was a well-developed man, with no other external markings. When the upper part of the skull was removed there were dark clots of blood but otherwise it was healthy. Cause of death was given as compression of the brain caused by meningenal haemorrhage due to the violence that caused the bruise. He confirmed that it would not need a great deal of violence, but was not caused by a blow from a fist. It could have been caused by the point of a boot or clog but there did not seem to be sufficient injury for this, nor was the bruise the right shape.

PC Bottomley said that he had decided that Spencer was drunk, even though he was told that he'd been knocked down. It never occurred to him that this might have injured him until later when Spencer was transferred from the police cells to the hospital. One reason why Bottomley might have considered Spencer merely drunk

St Luke's Hospital which used to be the Old Workhouse. The Author

was that Spencer was well known to the police. He had regularly been before the magistrates for drunkenness with or without the fighting, and had often been committed previously to the House of Correction for these offences.

However, Michael Henry, a thirty-six-year-old labourer, of Kirkgate was brought before magistrates J Crosland and T Topping, charged with manslaughter.

The Chief Constable, Mr J Morton, who applied for a remand, said the charge was a very serious one indeed. The deceased man was locked up on Saturday afternoon on a charge of being drunk and incapable. There was not the slightest doubt the man had had a large quantity of drink. Information was given to the police that prior to Spencer being arrested he had been severely assaulted by some person and that person was Michael Henry. Henry was remanded in custody.

The trial took place on 1 December 1914 at the West Riding Assizes at Leeds Town Hall before Mr Justice Shearman. Michael Henry, described as a builder's labourer, surrendered to his bail on a charge of manslaughter. Mr Frank Beverley – instructed by Mr J Lewis Sykes – appeared for the prosecution and Mr Ackroyde

Edgerton Cemetery, Huddersfield. The Author

Simpson – instructed by Mr L F Senior – represented the prisoner who pleaded not guilty.

The facts of the case were repeated, with additional post-mortem information showing that following the blows by Henry, a clot of blood gradually formed with increasing pressure on Spencer's brain in the region of the frontal lobe which resulted in death on the following day at the Crosland Moor hospital.

The medical testimony showed that the life of the deceased could not have been saved, as the blood clot formed on the side of the brain opposite to the place where the slight bruise was visible.

His lordship said that whilst sympathising with the prisoner in his present position, the latter had no justification whatever for striking the deceased and he must go to prison for one calendar month, with hard labour. The local newspaper considered this a 'lenient sentence'.

Spencer was buried in Edgerton cemetery.

CHAPTER 29

A Complicated and Baffling Mystery 1915

He found the body lying on the bed with the throat cut.

I n 1915 sudden death was not unexpected – if you were a soldier serving at the front. But everyone was shocked when a soldier's wife was found dead in the quiet village of Honley. Alice Kaye had previously lived with her parents in Dodworth near Barnsley, but both were by this time dead. In 1908 she had married Ernest Kaye. Under her mother's will she received a fairly large legacy but that fact was not thought relevant to the case. Initially she and her husband had lived in Birkby but they had moved back to Honley to live in Berry Croft. Alice had several cousins living in Honley and the family appeared to be very highly respected in the district.

Ernest had enlisted the previous November as a private in the 10th Battalion, Duke of Wellington's West Riding Regiment. Both his parents had died when he was a child, so his aunt and uncle, Mr and Mrs Whitworth of 66 Grove St Huddersfield, had brought up Ernest and his sister. He was an apprentice in the plumbing trade but owing to an attack of rheumatic fever at the age of sixteen had to give the work up. He had been employed at Starkey's mill in Longroyd Bridge until the firm ceased to exist but then found work in the goods ware-house at Huddersfield railway station. That proved to be too heavy so he had eventually became a porter at Brockholes station. He had also worked for Messrs J H Conacher and Co. Three months previously he had been posted to France but his aunt had received a postcard in an envelope from him on the previous Wednesday in which he said the weather was very bad and that he was full of cold through 'sitting wet' so often.

Alice was expecting a baby and was almost at the end of her term. Rather than leave her alone, her aunt, Eliza Donkersley of 7 Scotgate Road, had been staying with Alice during the nights of the past five

"I HAVE DONE THAT MURDER AT HONLEY."

REMARKABLE CONFESSION READ AT POLICE COURT.

PRISONER COMMITTED FOR TRIAL AT THE ASSIZES.

Another stage in the Honley murder

Newspaper headlines from the Hudders-field & Holmfirth Examiner. Author's collection

weeks 'for company' as Mrs Donkersley put it. She went to the house in Berry Crofts as usual between 8.30 pm and 9 pm on Saturday and found that the door was locked and the blinds drawn. Knocking on the door, she called out 'Alice' but got no answer. A milkman, who had been to the house just previously, had also been unable to gain admission. Accepting the hospitality of a neighbour Mrs Donkersley stayed near the house all night and at intervals went to the door but found no change in the circumstances. About 10 am on Sunday Mrs Donkersley spoke to Frank Oldfield, a joiner and builder from Bradshaw Road, Honley and also related by marriage to Alice, to ask him what they should do. Mr Oldfield went to the house in Berry Croft and found that the thumb piece of the door handle was missing, as was the key. He borrowed a key from a neighbour and opened the door. He found the body lying on the bed with its throat cut.

Oldfield then informed the police. When the constable arrived, he and Oldfield searched through the house but could find neither a weapon nor the thumb-piece of the door handle. Police Sergeant Hanson went to the house and at once began to investigate the case. Dr Smailes examined the body and expressed the opinion that the wound could not have been self-inflicted and that the woman could not have lived more than a few minutes after it was inflicted.

The inquest was held at 10.40 am the following day at the Honley Wesleyan school. But Thursday's newspaper carried exciting news:

MURDER VERDICT AGAINST A LABOURER

Confession of guilt in the Honley Tragedy

The crime committed with a pocket knife

There was a sensational development in connection with the Honley tragedy last night. A man named Harry Thompson aged fifty-five a chemical labourer, employed at Messrs Read Holliday and Sons Ltd, and living at Bradley Old Lane, Bradley, surrendered himself to Detective Taylor of the Borough Police Force. Accosting Detective Taylor in Ramsden Street, Thompson asked to be taken to the police station. At the Borough Police Station it is alleged that he made a confession regarding the murder . . .

Eliza Donkersley was the first witness, telling the court why she had been at the house on Saturday night. She also stated that though:

> ... *she had never known 'for certain' that any person had been in the habit of visiting at Mrs Kaye's house until the Feast holiday week when a man went to the railings in front of her house and asked for Mrs Kaye. She asked him what he wanted her for and said that if the man left a message she would give it to Mrs Kaye and asked him what was his name. He said, 'Thompson.' She never saw the man again and did not know that he visited Mrs Kaye.*

After describing how they had got into the house she told the court:

> *When they got in they found that deceased's head was lying towards the foot of the bed with her feet on the pillow. Her knees were doubled up and her right hand was over her breast and her left hand was a little lower down on the breast. Her throat was cut. Both hands were clenched. She was fully dressed and her clothing was only slightly disarranged. A chest of drawers near the bed head was pulled away from the wall and the carpet with it. The house only contained one room and a cellar and there was no other disarrangement in the house. She and others looked all over the house for a weapon but could not find one. She had never heard deceased threaten to commit suicide and to her knowledge deceased had no enemies.*

Thompson was given the opportunity of questioning the witness but he said that he had nothing to ask her, nor did he ask questions of Frank Oldfield when he came to give his evidence, corroborating all that Mrs Donkersley had said.

The police explained what they had found at the house on Sunday:

> *The body was on the top of the* [bed] *clothes, the head being slightly inclined towards the right and the knees which were slightly drawn up were inclined to the left. The left hand was below the left breast and the right hand above the middle of the breast. He searched for a knife in the vicinity of the bed; around the room and in the coal place but could not find it. Apart from the chest of drawers there were absolutely no signs of a struggle. Deceased was wearing a little silk shawl and it was matted with blood. Immediately under the head there was a large quantity of blood which had soaked right through the bedding on to the laths of the bed but there was not a spot of blood in any other portion of the room. The only table knives in the house, two in number, had been used to prepare a meal, and bore traces of bread and butter. The table had been cleared but there were traces of a meal amongst the crockery on the sink-stone. A small basin and two plates had contained salmon, and there*

was an empty salmon tin on the sink-stone along with two pint mugs and a plate containing a small quantity of cheese. There was a red table cover on the table. The two chairs were drawn up to it, but there were no signs of the door key or the thumb piece of the latch.

A surprise stab

The severity of the wound was described by Dr W H Smailes who said that he found the body stripped to the waist. There was a transverse incised wound on the throat two and a half inches long and gaping to the width of three quarters of an inch and extending from a point a quarter of an inch to the left of the middle line across the throat to the right, parallel to the chin and border of the lower jaw and an inch below it. The right extremity of the wound was clean cut and the left extremity was forked, as if there had been two cuts. Just at first he thought that the wound was self-inflicted but upon feeling the depth of the wound he found that the main blood vessels on that side of the neck were completely divided, and the vertebrae was notched – a most unusual circumstance in cases of suicide. This pointed to considerable force having been used with a sharp instrument and indicated that death would be almost instantaneous. Had she committed the deed herself she would have had no opportunity of concealing the weapons. There were two small bruises on the left lower jaw; there were two small bruises about the size of a sixpenny piece. He would say that when he saw her shortly after noon she had been dead at least twelve hours. From the jagged appearance of the left extremity of the wound it was possible that there had been two stabs but the direction of the wound was such as would be taken by a self-inflicted stab by a right handed person. There were no marks on the arms, hands or chest. Apparently, there had been a surprise blow, which the deceased had not resisted.

The last time that the deceased was seen alive was when she was spoken to by John Edward Cousen, 17 Berry Croft, a power-loom tuner, who said that he saw Alice on Saturday afternoon between 1.30 and 2 pm and she was then in front of her house. He saw no one go to the house that day nor previously but during the holiday week in September he saw her with a man in Northumberland Street, Huddersfield. Last winter he saw her with a man at the Palace Theatre. He did not know the man and would not recognise him but on each occasion the man was an oldish fellow.

Prisoner's admission

The circumstances of the prisoner's surrender to the police were described by Detective Taylor, of the Huddersfield Borough Police.

Palace Theatre, now Chicago Rock. The Author

He said that at 9.10 pm on Monday night he was going down Ramsden Street, Huddersfield when a man whom he did not know, shouted to him. The man said, 'Oh, Taylor, I want you to take me to the Police Station.'

When asked, 'What for?' the man replied, 'Well, it's over the Honley job.'

Taylor took the man to the Borough Police Station and there, after being cautioned, he made the following statement, voluntarily:

> *I have done that murder at Honley on Saturday. I did it with a pocket-knife. I have known her over two years. I was mad when I did it. I did not know that she was dead when I left her. I have been allowing her four shillings per week for the past two years or thereabouts. She has introduced me to her husband as her brother. I thought she was a single woman. I have some letters at home which she has sent to me. I have thrown the knife and the door key away.*

That statement was taken down by Taylor in his pocket book in writing and signed 'Harry Thompson' by the man in the presence of Taylor and the Chief Constable. Thompson gave his address as 100

Bradley Old Lane, Bradley and added that he had been a labourer employed by Mr Mark Brook, contractor.

Throughout the hearing – which extended over three hours, Thompson, a powerfully built man with grey hair and wearing a dark suit and a cloth cap, sat in one corner of the classroom absolutely calm and unmoved, following the evidence closely.

In summing up, the deputy coroner said that he thought that the jury would probably consider that the evidence was quite sufficient to enable them to arrive at a verdict. From the appearance of the crockery, he said it would appear that two persons had partaken of a meal in the house. The medical evidence pointed to the wound not having been self-inflicted. Apparently from the evidence of the aunt, the deceased knew a man named Thompson. The jury occupied only a few moments in arriving at their verdict. They found that Alice Kaye was stabbed in the throat by Harry Thompson and returned a verdict of wilful murder against him.

Later that afternoon Thompson was brought before the magistrates at the County Police Court on a charge of murder and was remanded in custody.

By 18 November the husband had been recalled from France and was able to attend the hearing in the County Police Court. Abraham Booth (presiding) and Samuel Firth heard the case in which W R Ley prosecuted. The public gallery was filled, there being 'a full attendance at court, including many women'.

A suggested motive

Mr Ley said the case was extraordinary – the prosecution 'evidence rested almost entirely upon the full and detailed confession which the prisoner made when he gave himself up to the police'. But he insisted that police had made enquiries 'which had been as carefully and fully made as if there had been no admission on the part of the prisoner' but had still not found any evidence to support facts.

When the police went to the prisoner's lodgings in Bradley they 'found the woman's garments folded up in a bundle and on the top of them was a tab on which was written "These belong to the dead woman" or words to that effect'. They also found nine letters written to the prisoner by the dead woman, which had been sent between the dates of 26 September and 5 November. The letters showed that the woman was very much attached to the man. In them were many expressions of love and affection. They also went to corroborate the prisoner's statement that he had been allowing her money. She had been in receipt of the separation allowance (for soldiers' wives) from her husband as well. As regards the prisoner's story that he had known her for two years, it might or might not be true so far as the police enquires went to show.

The police merely had to confirm how the confession had been made, together with the later statement giving details of letters and bundle of clothes. Mr Ley continued: 'Unless the magistrates or the prisoner wish it, I do not propose to read these letters. The actual details do not affect the case in any way.' When the prisoner was asked, 'Would you like these letters to be read?' He replied, 'Not here, sir.'

Dr Smailes then gave evidence, confirmed that she was pregnant and that 'the child was practically a full-term child'.

Her aunt confirmed that the 'deceased always wore a wedding ring'. She also agreed that the bed valence and two aprons produced, were the property of the dead woman. But then Janet Dyson, wife of Thomas Herbert Dyson, mason of Bradford Road, Huddersfield where she had a fried fish shop, gave fresh evidence. She said the prisoner and deceased came in most Saturday nights. She was under the impression that they were going to be married and she had asked them about it. The pair were always on affectionate terms. But at 6.25 pm on Friday 5 November the prisoner called at her shop and appeared to be depressed. He told her he was cut up about the woman, that he 'broke a day off' work the same week and found she was a married woman. The prisoner told Mrs Dyson that he was at his wit's end and did not know what to do. He added that he should not have taken the house if he had known she was a married woman. According to the prosecution, that statement afforded a motive for the crime. If it was not true, he did not understand why the prisoner should say it.

Mrs Dyson said that Alice Kaye had never worn a wedding ring or said that she lived with her mother.

Martha Ann Denham, widow, of 98 Bradley Old Lane, confirmed Thompson had gone to live alone at Bradley Old Lane last May. She had seen the taller of two women on a photograph produced in court, several times at prisoner's house. She saw him last about noon on Saturday 6 November when he was standing near the window inside his house. At 12.30 pm the blinds of prisoner's house were drawn down and they had not been up since.

The final witness was Ernest Kaye who had returned from France. He had enlisted the previous November and last saw his wife on 17 June on Huddersfield station platform, but since then had been in France. The letters produced were in his wife's handwriting and the taller of two women in the photograph was his wife. The coat and trousers produced were his property.

However, when Thompson cross-examined him, Kaye denied all knowledge of Thompson.

'You say you have never seen me?'

'I have no recollection of having seen you. I can't recollect you.'

'You will swear to that?'

'Yes.'

'Didn't Alice introduce you to me on a Saturday night when the car from Sheepridge was about to leave Huddersfield for Honley?'

'No.'

'I say she introduced me to you.'

'Well, I can't remember it. When was it?'

'Did we shake hands or did we not?'

'No, I can't recollect seeing you or shaking hands with you.'

'Hasn't she fetched you from a club in Huddersfield on many occasions to go to the car when I was there?'

'No, I seem to remember something about a tall dark man with dark hair and moustache.'

'Did you never meet us coming from the Palace?'

'Never.'

'Did we not ask you where you were going and you turned round and came back to the car with us?'

'No, I can't recollect that at all.'

'You can't recollect anything?'

'I can recollect it all right – I don't seem to know you.'

The prisoner had no more to say, and produced no witnesses. He was committed to Leeds Assizes for trial on a charge of wilful murder. The hearing lasted only two and a quarter hours.

The final stage in the Honley murder case was reached on 29 November 1915, at Leeds. He appeared before Mr Justice Sankey, Mr Tebbs for the prosecution and Mr Rowan Hamilton represented the prisoner. The case was outlined again and Mr Tebb read out the last letter from Alice, dated 5 November:

> *Dear Harry*
> *Just a few lines to say I have not got it over yet, but I have had a great deal of pain, so I think if I were you I would not come up in the afternoon but come up by the six car and if I am like I am now I will meet you at the tram and then we can go for a short walk. You asked me to tell you the truth and I did so. It will be best for us both . . .*

He gave details of the last known movements of Thompson and Kaye, suggesting that the clothes left at Thompson's had been there some weeks and also said, 'When the prisoner was arrested there was found upon him a copy of the local evening paper published in Huddersfield containing an account of the murder.'

Thompson had changed his evidence:

He was, he said, a labourer and knew the deceased woman. He saw her on 6 November between noon and 1 pm the same night when she was in her ordinary health. He was on perfectly affectionate terms with her and had no quarrel. He left her between 5 and 6 pm the same night and she was then in her ordinary health and seated on the bed. He expected to see her again when she wrote to him during the following week.

Rowan Hamilton asked, 'When did you first hear of the murder or of her death?

'When I saw it in the paper.'

'When you read about it, was it a shock?'

'Yes, I was upset.'

'What made you give yourself up to the police?'

'Well, I thought I should be suspected for keeping company with her.'

'Had you done the murder?'

'Not at all. I did not realise what I was doing at the time I made the confession.'

Thompson was then cross-examined by Mr Tebb, when the prisoner said he was not working on the Saturday, but he worked on the Friday. Mrs Dyson's statement as to what he had said to her in the fish shop was true. He was very much upset about the discovery that deceased was a married woman. He found out she was a married woman about Honley Feast time.

Tebb asked, 'What did you understand she meant when she said in the letter of 5 November "you asked me to tell you the truth and I am doing so. It will be best for us both"?'

Thompson said that that referred to the confinement but did not expand further. Tebb continued his questions:

'Where were you on Sunday?'

'I went for a walk.'

'Did you go to work on Monday?'

'No.'

'Why?'

'Well I went to different places to get a drink.'

'Where did you see the paper in which you say you read the account of this murder?'

'I bought the paper in Huddersfield.'

'That was night time?'

'About five o'clock.'

'Where did you purchase the paper?'

'Near the Market Place, where they sell these papers.'

'Did you read the paper in the street or take it to some public house?'

'I read the paper in the Old Hat public house.'

'And you say you were upset?'

'Yes.'

'This was about 5 pm and I suppose you had had some drink?'

'Yes. I had had a drink or two.'

'And when you had read this paper did you leave this public house or stay there a few minutes?'

'I stayed a few minutes and then went home on the car to Sheepridge.'

Thompson went on to say that when he got home he wrote the label which had been referred to and which stated that the clothes belonged to Mrs Kaye. But Tebb had not finished. He was not convinced that Thompson had really confessed simply because he had read the account in the papers and wanted to know more.

'Why did you decide to give yourself up?'

'Well, I can't tell you, only I was very intimate with her and I thought I should be suspected of the job.'

'So you gave yourself up? Now what did the newspaper that you read state as to the murder?'

'It stated that there had been a murder or suspected murder at Honley.'

'And it gave her name and where she lived and did it give a few details as regards the murder?'

'It stated that she had been found with her throat cut. It stated that they had had to break the door open or something like that.'

'Was it your intention to make such a statement that they would be satisfied that you were the man who had done the crime?'

'I did make the statement but I did not know what I was doing at the time I made it.'

'The newspaper – did it say that the body had been found on the Sunday?'

'Yes, something to that effect.'

'How was it that you came to start your statement "I have done that murder at Honley on Saturday"? How did you know?'

'I knew that she had been found on the Sunday according to reading in the newspaper.'

'You said "I was mad when I did it". What did you mean by that? What was the "it"?'

'When I made the statement.'

'Then you said, "I have thrown the knife and the door key away"'?

'I did not know anything at all about that only what I read in the paper.'

Rowan Hamilton went on to show that the woman was 'very much in love with the prisoner'. He contended that the prisoner's distraught condition of mind when he saw from the newspaper that this woman had been foully done to death made it a natural thing for him to make the confession. He

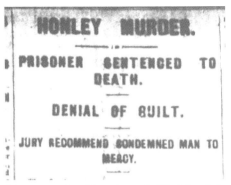

Newspaper headlines from the Huddersfield & Holmfirth Examiner. Author's collection

went on to say that men had made confessions of murder in the past when it had been shown that they had had absolutely nothing to do with the crime. It was for the prosecution, apart from the confession, to bring the murder home to Thompson 'which they had not done. There could be no question of reducing it to manslaughter, it must be either murder or acquittal.'

The judge agreed that it was murder or acquittal and that the prosecution had to prove 'beyond all reasonable doubt' – if the jury had a doubt they were not entitled to find him guilty. It was an unfortunate thing that the deceased was a married woman but this was not a court of morals. He agreed also that people do confess when not guilty. The jury must consider the state of mind, the fact that the

The entrance and walls of Wakefield Gaol, 2006. The Author

The few remaining gravestones of Moorbottom Cemetery. The Author

prisoner had just read the details in paper, that he had had a long friendship with the woman and just found out that she was a married woman. Thompson's main defence was that he was not responsible for his actions when he made the confession.

The jury retired for forty minutes before finding him guilty and unanimously recommended him to mercy.

The judge assumed the black cap, informing the prisoner, 'While you have not lost everything, you still have time to pray to God for forgiveness. He alone can comfort and help you and bring you safe home at last. The jury have recommended you to mercy and I will take care that the recommendation is immediately sent to the proper authority.'

Though the prisoner appeared more haggard than when he was before magistrates, he received the sentence 'quite unmoved.'

On 22 December Harry Thompson, aged forty-five, was executed at Wakefield prison. Pierrepoint was the executioner and death was instantaneous.

Alice Kaye was buried in Moorbottom Cemetery on 10 November 1915.

Bibliography

1. Books
Brian Bailey, *The Luddite Rebellion*, 1998, Sutton Publishing Ltd.
Kipling & Hall, *The Luddite Trail*, 1982.
Minter G & E, *Discovering Old Huddersfield*, Parts 1–5.
Redmonds, George, *Old Huddersfield 1500–1800*, Swiftprint.
Sykes RFE, *Huddersfield & its Vicinity*, 1898.

2. Archives
Parish register of Huddersfield & environs.
Nominal register of Wakefield Prison.
National Coal Mining Museum for England.
WYAS C493/K/2/1/3 Taylor notebooks.
Trade Directories: Baines, Kelly & White (1822–1899).
Census Returns 1841–1901 (Huddersfield area).
Calendar of Felons, York City Library.

3. Newspapers
Huddersfield & Holmfirth Examiner.
Leeds Mercury.
Huddersfield Chronicle.
Wakefield Express.

4. DVDs
Criminal Chronology of York Castle 1379–1867.
Chambers J, *Sentenced to Death & Transportation: Yorkshire 1830–1839*, 2005.

Index

People

Places